Weirdos in the Workplace

FT Prentice Hall
FINANCIAL TIMES

In an increasingly competitive world, it is quality
of thinking that gives an edge—an idea that opens new
doors, a technique that solves a problem, or an insight
that simply helps make sense of it all.

We work with leading authors in the various arenas
of business and finance to bring cutting-edge thinking
and best-learning practices to a global market.

It is our goal to create world-class print publications
and electronic products that give readers
knowledge and understanding that can then be
applied, whether studying or at work.

To find out more about our business
products, you can visit us at www.ft-ph.com.

Pearson
Education

Weirdos in the Workplace

The New Normal...
Thriving in the Age of the Individual

John Putzier, M.S., SPHR

FT Prentice Hall
FINANCIAL TIMES

An Imprint of PEARSON EDUCATION
Upper Saddle River, NJ • New York • London • San Francisco • Toronto • Sydney
Tokyo • Singapore • Hong Kong • Cape Town • Madrid
Paris • Milan • Munich • Amsterdam

www.ft-ph.com

Library of Congress Cataloging-in-Publication Data

Putzier, John, 1951–
  Weirdos in the workplace : the new normal— : thriving in the age of the individual /
John Putzier.
    p. cm.
  Includes index.
  ISBN 0-13-147899-0
    1. Organizational behavior. 2. Industrial relations. 3. Creative ability. 4. Executive
ability. I. Title.

  HD58.7.P88 2004
  650.1'3—dc22   2004053430

Editorial/Production Supervisor: *MetroVoice Publishing Services*
Executive Editor: *Jim Boyd*
Editorial Assistant: *Linda Ramagnano*
Marketing Manager: *Martin Litkowski*
Cover Design: *Nina Scuderi*

© 2004 Pearson Education, Inc.
Publishing as Financial Times Prentice Hall
Upper Saddle River, New Jersey 07458

The publisher offers excellent discounts on this book when ordered in quantity
for bulk purchase or special sales. For more information, contact:

**U.S. Corporate and Government Sales, 1-800-382-3419, corpsales@pearsontechgroup.com.
For sales outside of the U.S., please contact: International Sales, 1-317-581-3793,
international@pearsontechgroup.com.**

Printed in the United States of America

Third Printing, October 2004

ISBN 0-13-147899-0

Pearson Education Ltd.
Pearson Education Australia PTY, Limited
Pearson Education Singapore, Pte. Ltd
Pearson Education North Asia Ltd
Pearson Education Canada, Ltd.
Pearson Educación de Mexico, S.A. de C.V.
Pearson Education—Japan
Pearson Education Malaysia, Pte. Ltd

FINANCIAL TIMES PRENTICE HALL BOOKS

For more information, please go to www.ft-ph.com

Business and Technology

Sarv Devaraj and Rajiv Kohli
  The IT Payoff: Measuring the Business Value of Information Technology Investments

Nicholas D. Evans
  Business Agility: Strategies for Gaining Competitive Advantage through Mobile Business Solutions

Nicholas D. Evans
  Business Innovation and Disruptive Technology: Harnessing the Power of Breakthrough Technology…for Competitive Advantage

Nicholas D. Evans
  Consumer Gadgets: 50 Ways to Have Fun and Simplify Your Life with Today's Technology…and Tomorrow's

Faisal Hoque
  The Alignment Effect: How to Get Real Business Value Out of Technology

Thomas Kern, Mary Cecelia Lacity, and Leslie P. Willcocks
  Netsourcing: Renting Business Applications and Services Over a Network

Ecommerce

Dale Neef
  E-procurement: From Strategy to Implementation

Economics

David Dranove
  What's Your Life Worth? Health Care Rationing…Who Lives? Who Dies? Who Decides?

David R. Henderson
  The Joy of Freedom: An Economist's Odyssey

Jonathan Wight
  Saving Adam Smith: A Tale of Wealth, Transformation, and Virtue

Entrepreneurship

Oren Fuerst and Uri Geiger
  From Concept to Wall Street: A Complete Guide to Entrepreneurship and Venture Capital

David Gladstone and Laura Gladstone
  Venture Capital Handbook: An Entrepreneur's Guide to Raising Venture Capital, Revised and Updated

Erica Orloff and Kathy Levinson, Ph.D.
  The 60-Second Commute: A Guide to Your 24/7 Home Office Life

Jeff Saperstein and Daniel Rouach
  Creating Regional Wealth in the Innovation Economy: Models, Perspectives, and Best Practices

International Business and Globalization

John C. Edmunds
  Brave New Wealthy World: Winning the Struggle for World Prosperity

Robert A. Isaak
  The Globalization Gap: How the Rich Get Richer and the Poor Get Left Further Behind

Johny K. Johansson
  In Your Face: How American Marketing Excess Fuels Anti-Americanism

Peter Marber
  Money Changes Everything: How Global Prosperity Is Reshaping Our Needs, Values, and Lifestyles

Fernando Robles, Françoise Simon, and Jerry Haar
  Winning Strategies for the New Latin Markets

Investments

Zvi Bodie and Michael J. Clowes
  Worry-Free Investing: A Safe Approach to Achieving Your Lifetime Goals

Michael Covel
  Trend Following: How Great Traders Make Millions in Up or Down Markets

Aswath Damodaran
  Investment Fables: Exposing the Myths of "Can't Miss" Investment Strategies

Harry Domash
  Fire Your Stock Analyst! Analyzing Stocks on Your Own

David Gladstone and Laura Gladstone
  Venture Capital Investing: The Complete Handbook for Investing in Businesses for Outstanding Profits

D. Quinn Mills
  Buy, Lie, and Sell High: How Investors Lost Out on Enron and the Internet Bubble

D. Quinn Mills
  Wheel, Deal, and Steal: Deceptive Accounting, Deceitful CEOs, and Ineffective Reforms

Michael J. Panzner
  The New Laws of the Stock Market Jungle: An Insider's Guide to Successful Investing in a Changing World

H. David Sherman, S. David Young, and Harris Collingwood
  Profits You Can Trust: Spotting & Surviving Accounting Landmines

Michael Thomsett
  Stock Profits: Getting to the Core—New Fundamentals for a New Age

Leadership

Jim Despain and Jane Bodman Converse
  And Dignity for All: Unlocking Greatness through Values-Based Leadership

Marshall Goldsmith, Cathy Greenberg, Alastair Robertson, and Maya Hu-Chan
  Global Leadership: The Next Generation

Management

Rob Austin and Lee Devin
  Artful Making: What Managers Need to Know About How Artists Work

J. Stewart Black and Hal B. Gregersen
  Leading Strategic Change: Breaking Through the Brain Barrier

Management

Rob Austin and Lee Devin
Artful Making: What Managers Need to Know About How Artists Work

Dr. Judith M. Bardwick
Seeking the Calm in the Storm: Managing Chaos in Your Business Life

J. Stewart Black and Hal B. Gregersen
Leading Strategic Change: Breaking Through the Brain Barrier

William C. Byham, Audrey B. Smith, and Matthew J. Paese
Grow Your Own Leaders: How to Identify, Develop, and Retain Leadership Talent

David M. Carter and Darren Rovell
On the Ball: What You Can Learn About Business from Sports Leaders

Subir Chowdhury
Organization 21C: Someday All Organizations Will Lead this Way

Subir Chowdhury
The Talent Era: Achieving a High Return on Talent

James W. Cortada
Making the Information Society: Experience, Consequences, and Possibilities

Ross Dawson
*Living Networks: Leading Your Company, Customers, and Partners
in the Hyper-connected Economy*

Robert B. Handfield, Ph.d, and Ernest L. Nichols
Supply Chain Redesign: Transforming Supply Chains into Integrated Value Systems

Harvey A. Hornstein
*The Haves and the Have Nots: The Abuse of Power and Privilege in the Workplace…
and How to Control It*

Kevin Kennedy and Mary Moore
Going the Distance: Why Some Companies Dominate and Others Fail

Robin Miller
The Online Rules of Successful Companies: The Fool-Proof Guide to Building Profits

Fergus O'Connell
The Competitive Advantage of Common Sense: Using the Power You Already Have

Richard W. Paul and Linda Elder
Critical Thinking: Tools for Taking Charge of Your Professional and Personal Life

Matthew Serbin Pittinsky, Editor
The Wired Tower: Perspectives on the Impact of the Internet on Higher Education

W. Alan Randolph and Barry Z. Posner
*Checkered Flag Projects: 10 Rules for Creating and Managing Projects that Win,
Second Edition*

Stephen P. Robbins
The Truth About Managing People…And Nothing but the Truth

Ronald Snee and Roger Hoerl
*Leading Six Sigma: A Step-by-Step Guide Based on Experience with GE and Other
Six Sigma Companies*

Jerry Weissman
Presenting to Win: The Art of Telling Your Story

Marketing

Michael Basch
CustomerCulture: How FedEx and Other Great Companies Put the Customer First Every Day

Deirdre Breakenridge
Cyberbranding: Brand Building in the Digital Economy

Jonathan Cagan and Craig M. Vogel
Creating Breakthrough Products: Innovation from Product Planning to Program Approval

James W. Cortada
21st Century Business: Managing and Working in the New Digital Economy

Al Lieberman, with Patricia Esgate
The Entertainment Marketing Revolution: Bringing the Moguls, the Media, and the Magic to the World

Tom Osenton
Customer Share Marketing: How the World's Great Marketers Unlock Profits from Customer Loyalty

Yoram J. Wind and Vijay Mahajan, with Robert Gunther
Convergence Marketing: Strategies for Reaching the New Hybrid Consumer

Public Relations

Gerald R. Baron
Now Is Too Late: Survival in an Era of Instant News

Deirdre Breakenridge and Thomas J. DeLoughry
The New PR Toolkit: Strategies for Successful Media Relations

Strategy

Thomas L. Barton, William G. Shenkir, and Paul L. Walker
Making Enterprise Risk Management Pay Off: How Leading Companies Implement Risk Management

Henry A. Davis and William W. Sihler
Financial Turnarounds: Preserving Enterprise Value

To my wife, Loriann
for hanging in there with the ultimate weirdo!

CONTENTS

Foreword   *xv*

Acknowledgments   *xix*

chapter 1   How Did We Get Here, and Where Are
             We Going?   *3*

             As Goes the World, So Goes the Workplace   *4*

             The Age of the Organization Man (Stifling)   *5*

             The Age of Diversity (Tolerating)   *6*

             The Age of the New Economy (Accepting)   *8*

             The Age of the Individual (Rejoicing!)   *10*
             Good News/Bad News   *12*
             Why Are So Many High Performers So Weird?   *15*
             What Will This Book Do for Me?   *18*

chapter 2   Individuality from Soup to Nuts   *25*

             Blue Suit Bob   *26*

             A Boy Named Sue   *29*

             A Boy Named Sue (Part 2)   *31*

             The Devil Made Me Do It!   *32*

             Freedom *from* Religion?   *33*

Minimum Coverage (Part 1)   *34*

Minimum Coverage (Part 2)   *36*

Hoof-in-Mouth Hal   *37*

If You Want the Job Done Right!   *41*

Al Naturale   *43*

Al Naturale (Part 2)   *45*

Chatty Cathy   *46*

Walking Art   *48*

Somebody's Got to Do It!   *49*

What's It to Ya?   *52*

Abused and Confused   *54*

Abused and Confused (Part 2)   *56*

Got Milk?   *58*

Quid Pro Quo Pro (AKA Tit for Tat)   *59*

When Perception Ain't Reality   *63*

Ticks & Twitches   *64*

Public Affairs   *66*

Wanna Buy Some Cookies?   *69*

Carpal Tunnel Crapola   *71*

Is it Work, or is it Play.com?   *73*

The X-pense Account   *76*

The Two-Year Head Cold   *79*

The Customer is Not Always Right?   *84*

Pets are People Too   *87*

Helen the Hypochondriac   *88*

Human Billboards   *89*

Long Live the Confederacy!   *91*

System Tester Sam   *92*

Otto versus Oblivious   *96*

Feng Shui Phoebe   *97*

Circadian Charlie   *99*

chapter 3   What's IN with High Performers?   *105*

INdividualism   *106*

INdependence   *113*

INformation   *117*

                     INcentives   122
                     INnovation   129
                     IN Conclusion   135

chapter 4   Tools and Techniques to Change Others,
              Organizations, and Yourself   139

                     Behavioral Change Map   139
                     Organizational Change Map   153
                     AIM to Be Weird   159

chapter 5   Conclusions and Universal Truths   175

                     Conclusions   175
                     Universal Truths   176

About the Author   181

Weirdisms   183

Index   187

FOREWORD

Libby Sartain,[*]
Senior Professional in Human Resources
Executive Vice President and Chief People Officer
Yahoo! Inc.

A recent issue of *Fast Company* magazine had a picture of me next to a large headline that said "Act Normal." Anyone who knows me at all, upon reading that headline without reading the article ("She's Helping Yahoo! Act Normal"), would ask, "What does she know about acting normal?" The article was actually part of an entire feature on "The New Normal." It addressed, for the business world, the question of what do we do now—from dot-com boom to dot-com bust, to terrorism, to recession, to war, to whatever comes next? What do we need to know and do about competing, winning, and leading today? Is there

---

[*]Libby Sartain is responsible for leading Yahoo! Inc.'s global human resources efforts as Executive Vice President and Chief People Officer. Prior to joining Yahoo!, Sartain was Vice President of People at Southwest Airlines, a leading employer of choice. Sartain served as chairperson of the Society for Human Resource Management and was named fellow of the National Academy of Human Resources. She is the co-author with Martha Finney of *HR from the Heart: Inspiring Stories and Strategies for Building the People Side of Great Business* (AMACOM, 2003).

any "normal" in these uncertain times? And I would ask, if we aren't quite sure what normal is, how do we know what is weird?

According to Roger McNamee, who coined the term, *the new normal* is a time of substantial possibilities if you are willing to play by the new rules for the long term. In the new normal it is more important to do things right than to succumb to the tyranny of urgency. High standards for leadership, recruiting, investing, and due diligence are reemerging. There is room for large companies to invest in new technologies and develop new products and for innovative upstarts to change the world. For leaders, there will be new emphasis on finding and keeping top talent, and the key to success will be driving change and improvement and getting things done on a daily basis.

John Putzier is an expert on weirdness in the workplace. He knows how weird behavior can lead to innovation. He and I are kindred spirits of sorts. We met while both serving as volunteer leaders for the Society of Human Resource Management during my years at Southwest Airlines before I took the bold step to move to the Silicon Valley to join Yahoo! Inc., right in the middle of the dot-com bust.

We share a common interest in what it takes to make a company a great place to work. I was in the enviable position of heading the people function for a company frequently named as one of the best companies to work for in America and was sharing with my peers what I thought made Southwest Airlines a great work environment. John headed his own organizational behavior consulting firm, FirStep, Inc. with a mission of ridding the world of jerks at work. (I am not sure he is finished with that yet.) But we share similar visions about work and its role in life, human resource management as a profession, and other management and business perspectives. We know that light-heartedness, humor, and irreverence about work and life can make both more meaningful and fun.

But don't be fooled! Our philosophies are no-nonsense, and support the business agenda of the organizations that employ us. We know that now is one of the most exciting times to be a corporate leader. We have the opportunity to demonstrate like never before the true value in wise corporate stewardship, linking profitable, strategically sound business decisions with honor, trust, and hope. Fun and passion at work are essential for success and fulfillment. But that is not just Human Resources' job! It is everyone's job, including yours!

One of John's key principles is that every business leader must be a human resource manager, and that business success is driven first by common sense. We know that the companies we support have many talented people, who are capable of extraordinary results and want to give their best at work, if they can get past their fears, trust their leaders, and develop a sense of personal mission that is compatible with their respective organizations. And it's through these dedicated workers that the cumulative impacts of passion, imagination, dedication, and results can be experienced throughout your company.

To unleash the extraordinary efforts of your workforce, you must first believe this to be possible. Then, you must make sure that your people have the resources, support, and freedom to meet the challenges—or seize the opportunities—when they present themselves.

As we move into the future, our relationship with our people reinvents itself over and over again. Organizations in this brave new world of work are going to be forced to rise to this challenge not only by external market forces but also internally by the people themselves. In recent years, our workforce has experienced a steep decline in any trust they had for corporate America; they have seen and felt first-hand the demise of any real job security and the loss of hope in the so-called new economy.

Understand that our best performers and high potentials have not left the scene. They have been highly involved looking for the next big idea, looking for new markets and opportunities. The most talented workers are even more desirable than ever before—they're equipped to be true partners in helping our companies succeed. We had better have high-quality opportunities to offer them in return. And, we had better allow them to be themselves in their own unique way (i.e., high-performing weirdos in the workplace) or they will go somewhere else, where they can excel at being weird.

Weirdos in the Workplace is a fun read, but it is wrapped around some serious messages, which is why I like it. After reading this book, you will look at talent in a different way. You will have a greater understanding of how and when to make the distinction between someone being different for the betterment of the greater good, or just for the sake of making waves. You will have a keen awareness of how adding value is essential to truly finding oneself in the world of work. You will understand the difference between inclusion and discrimination, and when it might just be OK to discriminate.

During my school years, my friends often called me a "weirdo" to my face. And I am sure some call me that, and other names, behind my back now. In any leadership role, not everyone will be president of your fan club, and some days it feels that even when you do everything you can to make things great, your motives may be misunderstood or misinterpreted.

What you do to drive change may seem weird, different, or even bizarre to others. Don't let that stop you. And don't get bogged down by the day-to-day-ness of this kind of work. Keep in mind that you are entrusted with the hopes, desires, and expectations on both the corporate level and by the many employees who expect you to do the right thing. Let that trust be your inspiration!

Now go enjoy *Weirdos in the Workplace* and hopefully you can be one too!

ACKNOWLEDGMENTS

Hello! My name is John, and I'm a weirdo! (Hi, John!) That's the first (and last) step in my recovery program. My weirdness has served me well, but has also created some difficult challenges for me, for my wife, and for others in my life! As you may have read in the dedication, my wife, Loriann, did not want me to embark upon this project, but my weirdness took over, and I did it anyway. Not to spite her, but to surprise her, and more importantly, to prove something to us both.

Without boring you with a dissertation on my personal life, Loriann did not want to see me go through the trauma, both mental and physical, that I experienced during the writing of my first book, *Get Weird!*, and I am sure that she did not want to go through it either. But I learned a lot of painful lessons in that process and planned to overcome them this time around. (That's another story for another time.)

In effect, she was trying to protect me from myself, as she so admirably does so many times. So, I shelved the concept for a while, but it just wouldn't stay there. As my weird, creative comrades will concur, there are certain seeds that, once planted in a weirdo's brain, cannot be kept from growing. There are some who might say that this is because there is an abundance of fertilizer up there! Who says fertilizer is a bad thing? Again, another story for another time!

Whatever the reason, I could not hold it down any longer, so I decided to try to complete this project on the sly, on the side, and on the fly, in an effort to learn how to contain the stressful side effects, with the ultimate hope that I could spring it on her once I received an advance from a publisher. Money has a certain calming effect, ya know? After all, how else were we going to pay for that cottage on Chautauqua Lake? Debt and fear can be powerful motivators!

Well, I am proud to inform you that I dunnit! And I'm still married … yes, to Loriann! Which brings me to my first acknowledgement (long time comin', huh?), and that is to Loriann. Not just for staying married to me in spite of this sneaky little book, but for sticking with me through all my weirdness to date. It is said that one's strength is also one's weakness, and I know that my weirdness was endearing to her when we first met, but I am also sure that it can be equally taxing at times, and she handles it, and me, quite well.

As you will learn in reading this book, weirdos can be difficult people, and I am no exception. I admit it. Maybe this book is, in some weird way, an attempt to validate myself, or some type of justification for the burdens I place on the people around me. I know that I have to be reined in on occasion. You will better understand this phenomenon when you read about low self-monitoring and high self-efficacy later in the book. It can be a good thing and a bad thing at the same time. Yin and Yang have surrounded me all my life, including my corporate logo for FirStep, Inc. (*www.firstepinc.com*). (The "S" is a yin-yang.)

I am truly blessed to have family, friends, and colleagues who give me enough rope to swing to the edges of life, but not so much rope as to hang myself (yet!). At my best, this "edginess" is what makes me who I am as a writer, speaker, and business strategist and what differentiates me in the world of work. I now get paid to say things that I used to get fired for! So, thank you, God, for the weird brain you have given me, for those who have fostered it, and for the people around me who have even learned how to appreciate it!

OK, enough about me and my problems! On the business and professional side of things, I would be remiss if I did not thank a number of people who were critical players and partners in getting this book into your hands. To begin, I am deeply grateful for the contributions of Eugene K. Connors, Esq., termed by America's Leading Business Lawyers as among the top 15 management-side employment and labor attorneys in Pennsylvania, who provided a unique blend of legal and practical insights into several of the more off-beat cases.

The unique thing about Gene is not only his sense of humor and writing style, but the fact that he didn't even send me a bill! Gene is known for being able to guide companies on how to best balance employer–employee needs to eliminate employment concerns while maximizing management options. Just what we needed for this book!

On a "weirder" note, you need to know just how Financial Times Prentice Hall became the publisher of this book. Long story short, I was one day away from signing with my former publisher. The contract was sitting in my in-tray, awaiting my return from a business trip, and while on a flight home from Atlanta to Pittsburgh, I just happened to be assigned a seat (thank God for that first class upgrade!) right next to Ms. Emily Williams Knight, CIS Marketing Manager for Prentice Hall.

After the cursory "Hello, what do you do?" schtick, we got into more depth about book writing, publishing, etc., and when I told her that I was just finishing my second book, she thought that there might be something to this chance meeting. After a couple of emails and a referral, I was forwarding my manuscript and proposal to Mr. Jim Boyd, Executive Editor of Financial Times Prentice Hall, and within a matter of days, we had a deal! Who says big publishers are slow? So, THANK YOU, Emily and Jim!

And Jim, thank you for making me a better writer. Jim has a way of communicating tough love that doesn't hurt (too badly). I am deeply indebted to all the pre-publication reviewers to whom you sent my manuscript, and to them for having the backbone and talent to give me the whack on the side of the head I needed to make a good book even better. Even though it required a heck of a lot more work, in a very short amount of time, both I and the book are better for it. Thank you!

That should do it! Unfortunately, there are always so many others who contribute to a "successful" book *after* it comes out, but I cannot thank them here because I don't even know who they are yet. So, for all of you who invite me to appear on your talk shows, publish my articles, hire me to speak, etc., thank you in advance!

But most importantly, thank YOU for buying and reading *Weirdos in the Workplace*, because nothing else matters until you, the reader, make it happen. ENJOY!

How Did
We Get Here,
and Where Are
We Going?

Chapter 1————

HOW DID WE GET HERE, AND WHERE ARE WE GOING?

A WEIRDO IS ANYONE NOT LIKE YOU! Sad, but true. Let's get this straight right from the start. Which is one reason why there seem to be so many of them out there. Have you noticed that you can't even count on people who look like you to be normal (like you) anymore? It's every man (or woman) for himself these days.

> **A Weirdo is anyone not like you!**

Whatever happened to the good old days when people just came to work, did their jobs, kept their mouths shut, and didn't rock the boat? And you could count on them coming back the next day, and the next day, and doing it again and again until they got a gold watch and retired. And why is career success becoming so difficult for so many?

Why have workers and workplaces become so weird? Granted, the older we get, the narrower our definition of normal becomes, but it's more than just perception. Something is changing, and it's not just our perception. So what is it? What's the world coming to?

As Goes the World, So Goes the Workplace

The answer to these questions is that *the workplace is a microcosm of society.* The more aware you are of issues in modern society and culture, the more you can become a foreseer of workplace trends and challenges. It's absolutely fail-proof, and history proves it.

But before we go into a history lesson, it's important to understand that society, organizations, and individuals *all* follow a similar adaptive progression that can be captured in the acronym STAR: **S**tifling, **T**olerating, **A**ccepting, **R**ejoicing—particularly when it comes to major cultural shifts, which is what we are talking about here. It may happen at differing speeds, but the steps never change.

Think about it. When a change is thrust upon you that you do not initiate, nor that you want, isn't your first response to attempt to stifle it, to deny its relevance or its validity? But, once you realize that it is here to stay, you have to learn to tolerate it. That's just natural human adaptation. Eventually, if and when you realize it isn't going to kill you, and that you can't make it go away, for your own good, you must learn to accept it. It's a new status quo. A new normal!

It's the *R* in the STAR progression, however, that is the most difficult for most people, and must be set as a conscious goal before it can be accomplished. That is, to eventually learn to embrace the new reality and to find a way to actually capitalize upon it for you and your organization's own benefit and success. It's at this point that you and those around you can actually rejoice and succeed in the new reality. It's not easy, and it may not always be possible, but it is always advisable and desirable.

Now, the history lesson. Let's see how this STAR progression and the fact that *"As goes the world, so goes the workplace"* has been proven over time, and where it is taking us.

The Age of the Organization Man (Stifling)

Let's stroll down memory lane for a moment. It was post-World War II when we saw the advent of the "The Organization Man."[1] There was even a book by that title. If there was ever a period of time that exemplified the opposite of what we are seeing today, this is it. The key to success in the '50s and even the '60s was to conform, to blend.

> *If two people in an organization agree on everything, one of them probably isn't needed*

To be the epitome of the Organization Man not only meant adorning the traditional IBM white shirt and tie, but also required a white face, and a set of testicles. It wasn't considered even remotely discriminatory to hire and promote only white men for the "important" jobs, nor was it considered abnormal to require them to look and act alike, even if they didn't think alike. Organizations were run like an extension of the military, dominated by white men, and no one complained.

Life was good, at least for them, or so they thought. And, in fact, it was probably an appropriate organizational model for the time. Much was accomplished in this period, regardless of how it may look in hindsight. Which is the point. It's all relative. It doesn't matter if you agree with reality, it is reality! You can go back as far as you want in history, and this principle applies (slavery, suffrage, prohibition, etc.).

Yes, in 20/20 hindsight, the Age of the Organization Man was a period of severe stifling (on the STAR progression), but back then, creativity was not as valued a commodity as loyalty and harmony. Creativity and innovation, if and when it existed, came from the top (executives), from outside (the military, NASA), or from well-defined, controllable departments (R&D centers). Everyone else checked his or her opinions at the door, toed the company line, and did what they were told, hopefully until retirement.

---

1. *The Organization Man*, by William H. Whyte, New York: Doubleday, 1956.

Team building was somewhat of an oxymoron because in an environment where everyone agrees whether they agree or not, teamwork is confused with harmony. Going along and getting along were the overriding characteristics of a team player. In fact, there was no such thing as team dynamics and team development during this era. It wasn't needed!

Managing was easy as well. Imagine how easy it would be to be a manager if everyone looked, acted, and thought like you. Imagine if "being easy to manage" was considered a core measure of competency. Imagine if you had no one asking for special rights or privileges. No wonder they loved the status quo. But then things began to change.

The Age of Diversity (Tolerating)

Here come the '60s and '70s! Civil Rights. Hippies. Anti-war protestors. Social and political activists and militants. Presidential impeachment. Self-indulgent baby boomers entering the workforce. Drugs, sex and rock and roll. Feminism. Birth control. Legalized abortion. School busing. Affirmative Action ... and the list goes on. Remember, "As goes the world, so goes the workplace."

> *If opposites attract, then why do birds of a feather flock together?*

Take a look at this list of social phenomena and think about how all of these trends combined would have impacted the workplace during this period. This was an age of forced tolerance for forced diversity. It was not an organizational strategy. It was an organizational tragedy...for the traditionalists!

Need I say more? This is when the Organization Man lost his mind. The laments of the day were, "The work ethic is dead!" and "You just can't get good help anymore!" Managing became a nightmare because managers actually had to manage—that is, to make distinctions and difficult decisions, and they just didn't know how to do it. And they didn't *want* to do it! *This was the advent of weirdos in the workplace*, but at this point, it was just a bunch of square pegs in round holes, and it hurt! It wasn't accepted; just barely Tolerated.

There were Equal Opportunity and Affirmative Action, Age Discrimination in Employment, Americans with Disabilities, the Veterans Readjustment Act, and employment legislation out the wazoo. The multitude of laws requiring organizations to open their doors to *diversity* created great conflict and confusion. And remember that diversity was defined in strict legal terms called "protected classes": minorities, women, the disabled, and other clearly definable groups.

The sad irony was that equal opportunity measures were actually an insult to those for whom the laws were supposed to benefit. They didn't seem to realize that not all blacks think and act alike, not all women think and act alike, and so on. It was both simplistic and difficult at the same time.

Organizations hired specialists to work the numbers, called *compliance* officers (I know because I was one!), more to stay out of trouble than to advance the cause of diversity. It was compliance, not benevolence. Personnel became Human Resources. The glut of regulations also created a multitude of bureaucracies and bureaucrats. And lawsuits proliferated.

But, because this was such a new phenomenon, and it was forced, and still not accepted, these diverse groups learned that, to succeed, it was necessary to continue to try to "blend in" because the Organization Men were still holding the positions of power, and they detested and resisted this invasion of their sacred inner sanctum. They worshiped homogeneity, but were surrounded by heterogeneity. They idolized harmony, but were faced with conflict.

Women tried to become men (behaviorally back then). African-Americans tried to act white. Even WASP male baby boomers and former hippies like me tried to talk the talk and walk the walk of the traditionalists, not just to get along, but to get ahead. And it was pain-ful...for everyone!

And it never really worked. It worked in terms of opening the front door to formerly ostracized and alienated groups, but the doors to the boardroom, the executive conference room, and other circles of influ-ence remained closed, and the same agenda remained in place, but now with some new players on the field.

Eventually, as the economy soured in the '80s, the traditional value of loyalty, which was an icon in the Age of the Organization Man, was forced out the window. And ironically, it was initiated by the Organiza-tion Men. When push came to shove, reductions in force, and other downsizing initiatives ruled the day, and sent a chilling new message to the next generation of workers that it's every man for himself now. Diversity was not only here to stay, but now the economy required some tough choices to be made.

And now the rest of the story.

The Age of the New Economy (Accepting)

Welcome to the '80s and '90s. The last of the Organization Men were retiring or cashing out with golden parachutes, severance plans, early retirement incentive programs, and other ways to escape the reality that diversity and technology were not

> *Even a dead body will move in a river that is flowing*

only here to stay, but were coming of age. Although technology was not the primary driving force behind the exodus of the Organization Man, it was a compounding factor. Added altogether, going to work was no longer fun, and there was no turning back. There were only two choices, accept it or leave it. And leave it many of them did.

In the '80s there were still significant pockets of traditionalists in positions of power and in some of the stalwarts of industry, but baby boomers and other new workers were beginning to acquire greater power, not because they deserved it, particularly in the minds of the Organization Men, but because there was no choice. It wasn't by design, but by default. Who else was going to succeed them?

And, as we moved into the '90s, power was no longer rooted solely in position, but also in knowledge and expertise. Power now came with rare and valued talent and skill. New age techies and other high-achievers and talented individuals started to rule the roost, even if it was only departmental. Some weirdness was becoming an accepted cost of doing business and making money.

Combine the so-called new economy with the dot-com boom and the severe shortage of technical and other talent, and companies were now looking purely for talent, and didn't care what color, shape, or size it came in. Diversity almost became a non-issue because you could be purple with two heads and if you had talent, you had job offers.

It actually got to the point that almost anyone could succeed if they could fog the mirror, because organizations were suddenly desperate for warm bodies. And, because demand outweighed supply, knowledge workers and rare talent were now in the driver's seat for the first time in the history of organizations. And they capitalized on it.

Better offers were streaming in, new companies were being formed right and left, stock options were being handed out like candy, and the new worker went wherever the money and opportunity took him or her. Loyalty was now directed toward a profession, not an organization. Free Agent Nation had been born. Employees could truly become owners, even at the entry level.

And guess what these new workers were accused of? Being disloyal! If it weren't so pathetic it would be funny. But more importantly, with this new era also came new perks, privileges and prerogatives ranging from flex time to casual attire to actually having fun at work.

Blasphemy! The values of loyalty and harmony were now being super-ceded by the values of creativity and innovation. Ideas and results ruled the day!

This period represented a major transition in the world of work. Regardless of the fact that the so-called new economy may have been a flash in the pan, and that workers may never be "in charge" to the degree they were (which I predict will be true again), there was a new acceptance and a growing awareness of the value of diversity. But now it was going way beyond the traditional, legalistic definition of diversity to become The Age of the Individual.

The Age of the Individual (Rejoicing!)

It is coming. In fact, it is already here, but many organizations just haven't figured it out yet, or may still be hoping it will go away. Forget about it! Look around. And don't forget, "*As goes the world, so goes the workplace.*" New workers got a taste of what it is like to be appreciated for their individual value, and demonstrated how hard they will work and

> **There's no "I" in team, but there ain't no "we" either!**

how much they will sacrifice for an organization in which they have a stake and that rewards them accordingly. The work ethic is not dead; it has just been redefined.

In the Age of the Organization Man, the concept of teamwork was irrelevant. In the Age of the Individual, teamwork isn't irrelevant, but it is becoming marginalized, particularly where high performance and rare talent is concerned. Whoever coined the phrase, "there is no 'I' in team," didn't seem to notice that "there ain't no 'WE' either!"

If societal trends predict workplace trends, you don't have to look very far to see where we are going. From reality TV, to "An Army of

One," to professional sports, to style and fashion, to music and entertainment, the individual predominates, particularly if that individual is a star, or thinks he is. Standing out is far more important than fitting in, and the rewards are getting greater and greater.

Think about it. Even in team sports, the individual has become king. It may take a team to win a championship, but it's the individual who is inducted into the hall of fame. It's the individual whose records are remembered. It's the individual who breaks them. It may take a team to play a game, but your star scorer can't score unless she has the ball. Teamwork and the concept of free agency do not mix well.

So why and how can we rejoice in the Age of the Individual? Well, aren't you one? It doesn't mean that people don't still pull together and pitch in for each other. It doesn't mean that we still cannot accomplish more, and be more creative as a group. What it does mean is that organizations must now learn to identify, recognize, and reward their stars, shift their focus and emphasis on individual achievement and on finding, attracting, motivating, and rewarding as many of them as they can. It also means the end of catering to the middle and wasting excessive time and resources trying to teach a rock to swim. It's not an option if you strive to thrive in the Age of the Individual.

Understand that when you hire superstars, you do not have a team. You have a collection of individuals. It's the cold, hard truth. And it isn't necessarily a bad thing, as long as you have them doing what they should be doing. Ask any high performer what they think about depending on others for their success (i.e., a team), and in their moment of truth they will tell you quite bluntly that they would prefer to go it alone. You will learn more about this concept of "self-efficacy" later, so hold that thought.

Let's face it, most Americans are *not* inherently team players. We are not a collective society. Asians are collective. Americans are rugged individualists. We were founded by the malcontents who left the flock. It's just not in our culture to rely on others unless we have to. People will play the game and play along if it is necessary for them to meet their goals, but they feel stifled. Because they are!

Don't get me wrong. It's not like they want to work in a cave. They still want and need others as resources, sounding boards, and comrades, and they will instantly become a cohesive team in a crisis situation, but they do not want to be shackled (stifled) by being forced to defer to a team or a task force on something that is their true forte. Why?

Because in the Age of the Individual, the burning question inside each person is continually, "What's in it for me?" That's not the ethic we saw in the Post WWII era of the '50s, nor is it necessarily mercenary or narcissistic, but it is a new normal for the realities of today's world. And today's world is where we are living. Like it or not, it is what it is. And this is your wake-up call!

Good News/Bad News

Today's high performers have a free-agent mentality. Even those working for large corporations think and act like entrepreneurs. But the concept is not entirely new. Did you ever hear of Einstein participating on a quality circle team? Did you ever see Edison engaged in a group hug or team-building exercise? I don't think so! Geniuses and rare talent don't do well on teams. Never have; never will.

But now they rule, and they can even rule within organizations, if we let them. They must no longer be confined to working in R&D centers, skunk works or as sole proprietors. And traditional team members don't really like them. So why punish everyone, including yourself?

Even where artistic and creative genius *requires* working together, it's like oil and water. Look at how many rock bands and other performing arts groups, even the most successful ones, break up because of personality differences, clashes in creative concepts, and other non-team-like behavior. Many eventually decide to go out as soloists instead. This isn't really new, but it is becoming more prevalent in society and therefore in the workplace, thus making it necessary to learn how to embrace it in the most productive and profitable manner possible.

Those who know me already know that I not only respect weirdness, but actually encourage it. You also know that my respect for weirdos lies in the assumption that their weirdness is rooted in brilliance, high performance, rare talent, or some added value to an organization and/or to society; that they have tapped their "natural weirdness," the very essence of why they were added to the human gene pool. But weirdness knows no boundaries.

There are also weirdos who not only bring nothing of value to the game, but are actually a drain, and whose weirdness should not be fostered or even accommodated. We're talking about the difference between an Albert Einstein and a Charles Manson; a Martin Luther King and an Adolf Hitler. Although they were all weirdos in their own right, that does not necessarily mean they all added value to the world. To quote Albert Einstein, "the difference between stupidity and genius is that genius has its limits."

The point is that some weirdos are good, some are bad, and some are just an annoyance. Some add incredible value to the world, while others are merely a painful lesson to the rest of it. Some deserve to be loved, some should just be left alone, and others need to be lost forever. You will see all three categories in the cases that follow.

The goal is to win the winners, lose the losers, and learn how to tolerate or relocate those in the middle; but the real challenge is to know which are which, and what to do with them once you know. It's time for organizations to get tough about the deployment of human resources. Not everyone's weirdness deserves to be accommodated.

Exalting the Age of the Individual is a double-edged sword. On the one side, it can offer incredible opportunity and rewards to the best and the brightest, but it also requires us to bite the bullet when one's individuality offers nothing or even detracts from the greater good.

Think about it. What modern technology company wouldn't love to hire the next Thomas Edison? What sports team wouldn't jump at a chance to violate their salary cap to recruit just a few Michael Jordans or Tiger Woods? What art school wouldn't give their left ear for a contemporary Van Gogh or Michelangelo? What recording label wouldn't sign a bazillion dollar deal with the reincarnated Elvis? (I think one already did.) But once they got them, would they know what to do with them? And could they tolerate the wild eccentricities that can go along with the manifestation of their genius? In the Age of the Individual, we must learn to do so.

Traditionalists and bureaucrats refer to our society and its organizations as a melting pot. I prefer to think of it as a stir-fry, or a tossed salad. No one stands out in a melting pot. In a melting pot, everything is just fused into an indistinguishable blob. In a stir-fry or tossed salad, each individual component maintains its uniqueness, and contributes to the overall experience without losing its distinctive strength or identity. You can still see and taste the red tomato. You can still see and taste the green pepper. After all, you wouldn't put a bunch of salad fixings into a blender would you? Similarly, there are some things you would never put into a salad or a stir-fry, but they would be perfect in some other dish.

And that's the point! Everything and everyone has its place, but not everywhere! And, wherever that is, people want and need and deserve to retain their uniqueness. The same is true of organizations. You may not stand out, or excel, in one job or company or industry, but in another, you may develop into a real winner. Same person, different context; same vegetable, different dish. And it's up to the individual *and* the organization to participate in this journey.

That's why you will find tools and techniques in Chapter 4 that address this issue from all possible perspectives (changing others, changing organizations, and ultimately changing yourself).

The bottom line is that the world of work has changed, never to be the same again. From the advent of diversity and equal opportunity in the '70s, to the tech-nerd boom of the '90s, to the increased emphasis on political correctness and hyper-sensitivity of today, no one seems to know exactly how to act, or even *if* to act without fear of retribution or persecution. Vanilla has become the safe flavor of choice in many organizations today. And that has to change. It will change.

Please note, however, that in order to maximize and capitalize on this new mindset, both individually and organizationally, does not imply a new laissez-faire management style. With an increasingly exaggerated emphasis on "tolerance of anything and anyone" rooted in a new carte blanche "non-judgmentalism," combined with the new desire for "freedom without responsibility" with the overarching goal of attaining "self-esteem and fulfillment at any cost," you have a recipe for disaster. Weirdness for weirdness' sake is not the goal of a healthy society or organization.

The perceived politically correct need to treat everyone "equally" has resulted in the institutionalization of mediocrity and to the spinelessness of decision-makers. The era of the meritocracy (i.e., an organization in which one's success or failure is dependent upon his/her contribution and value) is long overdue, which exemplifies the underlying purpose of this book: to recognize, value, and foster the beneficial side of weirdness, while putting the brakes on "anything goes at anyone's expense." It's time to get real!

Why Are So Many High Performers So Weird?

Since understanding high performers is one of our goals, let's learn more about what makes them tick. We will go into much greater depth and detail on this subject in Chapter 3, "What's IN With High-Performers?," but for starters, it will help to understand a couple of basic psychological concepts specific to rare talent.

> *Everyone behaves perfectly rationally, from their point of view*

Many high-level thinkers, creative types, geniuses, and results-oriented individuals are low in something called "self-monitoring" behavior. In other words, they do not look in the mirror and ask themselves, "How do others see me?" They don't care! It rarely even enters their mind. They focus almost exclusively on one, narrow area of their expertise or their interest to the potential detriment of how the rest of the world may perceive them.

I admit that I have been as guilty as anyone of this so-called shortcoming, resulting in the occasional social faux pas. I have even rationalized it afterward by saying things like, "I wasn't really looking for new friends anyway." Rejecting others before they reject you is a form of self-defense and self-preservation. You will see this behavior in many individualists, and particularly in those who can "afford" to be different later in the book.

Some high-profile, easily recognizable examples of successful low self-monitors include the historic figures we've already mentioned, like Albert Einstein and Thomas Edison. But there are plenty of more contemporary weirdos like pop-singer Michael Jackson, the legendary Elvis, shock-jock Howard Stern, and even Herb Kelleher, long-time former CEO of Southwest Airlines. I'm sure you can think of many more in everyday modern life.

Some are respected and even admired, some are disdained, but all are highly accomplished, celebrated, and rewarded in their respective fields and equally odd and curious in many ways. Ironically, they succeed both in spite of and because of their low self-monitoring behavior. Isn't it strange how we are rewarding the most antisocial and perceptually abnormal among us? This is a key principle for you and your organization to understand in order to be able not only to tolerate, but to maximize the value of rare talent.

Traditionally, we think of actors, artists, athletes, and scientific geniuses as the most stereotypical examples of brilliant or talented, but bizarre individuals. But today, that same human enigma is penetrating the everyday workplace. In some cases, the weirdness may not even be exhibited on the job or even in appearance, but rather after hours in the form of weird hobbies, diversions, perversions, or other kinky outlets pursued to fulfill some latent, unsatisfied need.

Case in point: Google, the highly acclaimed web-search engine company, is a case study in savvy management, a company filled with cutting-edge ideas, and an anomaly in the here today, gone tomorrow world of digital technology. Google spends more time on hiring than on anything else. They look for young risk-takers. They define smart as, "Do they do something weird outside of work, something off the beaten path?" They believe that this translates into people who have no fear of trying difficult projects and going outside the bounds of what they know. They do not fear experimentation or change, but initiate it instead. They live and work outside the box.

But is it an employer's business to concern itself with employees' private lives? It isn't, unless it impacts job performance, the business, co-workers, and/or customers, in which case, it does become the employer's business and at which time the complexities of managing become immense. It also takes courage and creativity to do it right. You will see quite a few examples of this in the upcoming case studies, from the commonplace to the bizarre.

Another psychological commonality of high-performers is something called "self-efficacy" (also called internal attribution), which means that many of these "types" perceive themselves as having greater control over their lives and the lives of others than the average person. They rarely see themselves as victims of circumstances. Rather, they are usually the perpetrators of circumstances. They have a greater than usual tendency to "attribute" success or failure to their own actions rather than to external factors.

They accept responsibility, grab it by the horns, and find it next to impossible to conceive or concede that they may not have, or deserve, complete control. They can be boat-rockers, rebels, and malcontents. This is a wonderful and valuable attribute for an organization that rewards results and change. But it is a not-so-great attribute for those who do not share these traits, or have to work with, for, or over them—especially in situations in which they do not or should not have control. Again, you will see some examples of these in the upcoming cases, as well.

In any event, they *can* be dealt with, managed, and even capitalized upon. There's energy there that can be directed to awesome ends. That's exactly why some weirdos can be a blessing in disguise. The key is to know who they are and how to realize their value by not stifling it.

By the time you finish this book, you will be able to identify where, when, and how to focus your attention on unusual workplace behaviors based upon whether they have relative value or potential to the organization. You will be able to recognize alternative approaches and to select one most appropriate to you and your organization's success. And ultimately, you will have an increased understanding, acceptance, and appreciation for the ever-changing world around you, be able to see it coming, and hopefully be on the road to tapping your natural weirdness to become a more valuable member of the Age of the Individual.

What Will This Book Do for Me?

Weirdos in the Workplace will change the way you think and act about worker behavior, and will empower you to take appropriate action where necessary. You will learn that it is high time to recognize that discrimination is good!

> **Discrimination is good; discrimination is right; discrimination is necessary!**

The concept of discrimination has gotten a bad rap in recent years, and as a result, has been misinterpreted as a bad thing. If someone says you have discriminating taste, it's a compliment! It says that you are able to make worthwhile distinctions and decisions, and that is what is called for in the Age of the Individual. In fact, discrimination is not only good, but it is right and it is necessary if you expect to have any hopes of Thriving in the Age of the Individual.

So, why write a book that chronicles and analyzes weird behaviors at work? Well, there are several reasons. On the broadest, most prurient level, people just enjoy observing the human condition in its most rare or extreme form. Look at what sells on radio, TV, and the movies! Think of it as a form of societal/organizational voyeurism, like peeking at an auto accident, or watching reality TV. The cases alone make for a fun, and sometimes distressing read.

On a more focused and pragmatic level, however, since most of us have to spend over half our waking hours working with and for other people, it could come in handy to have a handbook or reference guide for survival and success. At one end of the spectrum, we need to learn how to understand and deal with those who cause us the most challenge, pain, or frustration, while at the other end, we need to learn how to accommodate, retain, and elicit excellence from the most powerfully talented of them all.

I recall in my earlier career as a corporate recruiter how candidates in job interviews would always say, "I like to work with people." I got so fed up with this moronic cliché that I got into the habit of following up with the question, "As opposed to what? Dogs?" I hope you like to work with people, because there are an awful lot of them out there! Regardless of your occupation, you can rarely escape human beings! And remember, a weirdo is anyone not like you. Thus, this book!

Finally, and most personally, once you realize the value of "tapping your natural weirdness," you will want to become a high-performing weirdo of worth, if you aren't already. Chapter 4 covers a concept called AIM, which represents the quest to identify and target the intersection of your Abilities, your Interests, and the Market.

Weirdos in the Workplace is an anthology of real-life case studies, showcasing some of the most bizarre behaviors at work, as well as some of the more common, but still challenging, weirdness that occurs in many workplaces, but for which most of us have no clear solution. It is, however, more than just a compilation of workplace horror stories, and it is *not just another management book.*

It is intended to transcend the pure human resource, management, and business genre to have general appeal and value to anyone who enjoys studying the human condition and anyone who wants to survive and thrive in today's world of work. In order to make this a truly experiential learning activity, I have collected and compiled a diverse portfolio of real-life workplace cases, which you can read, ponder, and then try to come up with your own solutions. Following each case is an expert analysis, accompanied in Chapter 4 by some universal tools and techniques that can be used to approach virtually any behavioral or organizational challenge.

It's a whole package. In Chapter 2, we start with the challenges created by individuals within organizations and offer some solutions. Then, in Chapter 3 we identify the five initiatives for creating a successful organization in the Age of the Individual. Then, in Chapter 4 we move to the dynamics and conditions of individual behavioral change, followed by a "how-to" tool and process for identifying, categorizing, and initiating organizational change. We will finish with a very personal section on how you, too, can become a high performer, which should be one of your goals while reading this book. As you will learn, the more you're worth, the more you can be weird!

In terms of the cases, as a general philosophy, it helps to understand a basic tenet that I teach students of organizational behavior: "contingency theory," which means that the answer to almost every human challenge is "it depends!" There is almost never just one solution, almost always a second right answer, and always more than one wrong answer, as well! That's what makes it so frustrating and so interesting at the same time. That's what makes management as much of an art as it is a science. It is also what makes it not for everyone. Managing today is not for the timid, the uncreative, or the lazy, particularly in the Age of the Individual.

Let's try a few on for size. Is body odor protected by freedom of religion? Which restroom should a trans-sexual use, particularly during their gender reassignment? May an employee moonlight as a stripper? What if the CEO is one of her patrons? Is it sexual harassment if I like it? Tough questions! Do you have solutions?

These are just a few of the unusual and challenging real-life case studies that are profiled and analyzed, but I have not overlooked the fact that there are more common, but almost equally as challenging people problems that can rear their ugly heads at work, so I have included those types of cases as well, such as the employee who buries porno movies on his expense report, the customer who's not always right and whose tirades are not worth the business, and the employee who is always poking at the system for attention.

Just chronicling bizarre and eccentric behavior in the workplace would be an amusing read by itself, but please understand that voyeuristic titillation is not the goal. Whether you agree with some of the weirdness that is becoming ever more evident in our world is not relevant here. This book is not a statement about religion, politics, or morality. It is a book about reality. It's a human resources serenity prayer.

Whatever your religious, political, or societal values and convictions, you cannot escape the reality that we are not all the same, and that society, particularly American society, is increasingly encouraging and even rewarding individuality and extreme behavior—a "new normal." That can be a good thing or a bad thing, which is a fundamental premise and message of this book.

The definition of "weird" is changing as well. The more weirdos there are, the fewer you actually see. For example, weirdos are more visible in Pittsburgh than they are in San Francisco. Why? Because the definition and perception of "normal" is much narrower in Pittsburgh than it is in San Francisco. Because weird has not become the norm in Pittsburgh.

And, like it or not, our laws, our media, our educational systems, and just about every other symbol and institution of our society are moving toward embracing this "new normal." The "normalization of weirdness" is in process right now, and if it is a given, we have no choice but to create new rules and tools to cope with it, deal with it, and to succeed because of or in spite of it. We cannot change reality. But we can change our reactions to it.

This book is not intended to be politically incorrect, nor offensive. In fact, I think you will find that it is actually just the opposite. It *is* honest and direct, which may be considered politically incorrect by some. But, once you understand that in the purest sense, everyone is a weirdo, including you; that the healthiest and most productive definition of diversity is individuality, not race, sex or some other governmental/regulatory definition; and that we must learn to make distinctions based on this new awareness and value of individuality, then you, the organization in which you work, and society at large will all be better for it.

And finally, the disclaimer.

Please note that the names of people and organizations, as well as some of the circumstances referenced in this book have been changed to protect their privacy. The analyses and commentaries are provided as general information and are not a substitute for legal or other professional advice. Neither the author, publisher, nor any other party to the publication or dissemination of this book may be held liable for the use, misuse, or misunderstanding of its content.

Individuality from Soup to Nuts

Chapter 2

INDIVIDUALITY FROM SOUP TO NUTS

(Cases and Analyses)

This section presents a series of real-life cases of behaviors and circumstances ranging all the way from just plain annoying to downright astonishing. Your challenge is to ask yourself what, if anything, would you do to address them?

If you are the type who does crossword puzzles with one finger on the answer page and the other on the puzzle, you may want to peruse the Tools and Techniques section (Chapter 4) beforehand, so you can have a leg up on the possible solutions. You will learn either way. In this case, it's not cheating, as long as you're learning!

If you are not that type, you can learn as you go by coming up with your own approaches and then comparing them to the expert analyses. Your approaches may very well be better than theirs! Remember, there are almost always several right answers in the world of weirdness.

The Tools and Techniques in Chapter 4 can also serve as a validation and reinforcement of what you have learned and provide you with a nice, succinct and universal summation of when, where, and how to approach virtually any human workplace challenge that might come your way!

Blue Suit Bob

Bob was a brilliant, high-potential, entry-level college graduate engineer, hired to work in the corporate headquarters design department of a leading Fortune 100, transnational manufacturing company. He was recruited on the campus of a prestigious engineering school, and made it through all his interviews with flying colors—primarily blue. He made the right appearance, wearing a standard-issue, conservative blue "interview" suit, blue-and-white power tie, and shined shoes, was clean cut, and came across as a "good fit" for this conservative, professional image-conscious organization. He got the job offer!

Bob was the type who kept to himself, spoke only when spoken to, and was clearly not a boat-rocker. Several months into his tenure, however, people started to notice that Bob was more than just the stereotypical introspective technical type, which they were all used to. The grapevine had him clearly labeled as a weirdo, not only because he seemed the stereotypical eccentric analytical, but particularly because he was never seen wearing anything but his original blue interview suit. Every day. Every week. Everywhere.

The dilemma was that he looked just fine. His attire was not only perfectly appropriate, but would actually be the quintessential "dress for success" look that every conservative corporate headquarters would love to clone. But please! Every day? Eventually everyone but Bob seemed to be aware of the situation, which eventually led to his manager coming to the Human Resources Department for guidance.

Appropriately so, the HR representative suggested a one-on-one, diplomatic, confidential discussion between the manager and Bob in which the manager should mention the situation, and the fact that, as a highly paid professional, he should be able to afford more than one outfit.

The manager did exactly that, to which Bob responded quite glibly, "But I do have more than one outfit! I have five!" They are all blue! Five blue suits, five white shirts, and five generic blue-and-white ties.

When the manager asked why he had such a "weird" wardrobe, Bob said that since his college placement counselor indicated that this was the most appropriate business attire, and since it apparently worked for him in the interview, he decided to just buy multiples of the same outfit. This way he wouldn't have to think about what to wear every day, could interchange them, and therefore apply his brainpower to more important things, like design engineering. Kind of like Einstein! What now?

Analysis

There are a couple of approaches one can take next with Bob. The first one is to do nothing—just leave him alone. In Chapter 4 (Tools and Techniques) you will find a decision-making tool called the Behavioral Change Map, which would have led you to this conclusion. Let's begin by looking at the first step of the Change Map (Figure 2.1) to see how it applies to Bob:

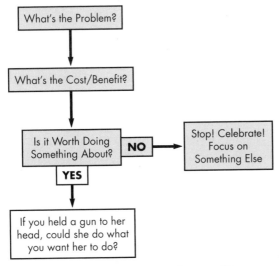

FIGURE 2.1   First step of the Change Map.

If you follow this logic and ask, "What's the problem?" you are really asking "What is it costing the organization?" or "What is the harm in Bob wearing blue suits?" It has no legitimate bearing on his co-workers, as long as he and his blue suits are clean, right? Is he reliable? Is he contributing? Is he doing his job? If so, the first approach is to focus on what Bob does for a living, and let him live.

There is a critical learning point here. Many people, and especially managers, obsess over things that don't deserve that much time and attention. In fact, many times the cost of intervention exceeds the cost of the perceived problem. This is where you learn to let go.

If, however, you determine that the cost/benefit of doing nothing *is* out of whack (customer complaints might be an example), then it would be within the right and purview of the employer to counsel again with Bob, and you might request that the next time he goes suit shopping, since no one can wear the same five suits forever, that he jazz up his wardrobe a bit.

You might even give him a complimentary copy of a dress-for-success book; or better yet, spring for a one-time personal fashion consultant to take him shopping. Most of the finer department stores offer this service for free, since they are going to make money on the purchases they select.

As you will discover throughout most of these cases, this is a case where maintaining one's self-esteem is essential. These counseling sessions should be conducted behind closed doors, and no one but you and Bob need to know that he is receiving such guidance. It is appropriate, however, to let Bob know that his co-workers (without naming or revealing anyone's identity) and your customers have lamented about his weird fashion statement, thus making it job-relevant, and not just a personal attack on his lack of good taste.

Finally, if he really wants to hold onto his Einsteinian logic for choosing his attire in the morning (i.e., requiring no thought), have the fashion advisor teach him how to label or color-code his wardrobe so that he automatically knows that if he chooses to wear suit "A" that there is a corresponding tie, belt, shoes, socks, etc., all labeled with a corresponding "A" so all he has to do is pick out all the "A" clothes and put them on. Left-brainers like Bob love this idea! Voilá! Solved!

Hey, you may even want try this yourself! Saves a lot of early-morning brainpower!

A Boy Named Sue

Sue was born Stu. A rough-and-tumble boy who became a rough-and-tumble man. He was a real man's man—a Harley-ridin'- beer drinkin'-ass-kickin' dude who had a knack for fixing engines to the point where he became a professional mechanic, working on the big rigs as a career.

But Stu had a secret. A deep, dark secret. For years, he yearned to be a woman. Not just a cross-dresser, but a full-fledged woman…physically. Eventually, his medical advisors agreed to support his need, determining that it was in his best interests, psychologically, to pursue the long and difficult process of "gender-reassignment" (i.e., a sex change).

Together, they petitioned Stu's employer and ultimately won approval for his surgery to be covered by the company medical plan. Stu was on the road to becoming Sue. So, what's the problem? As word got out and the process had progressed to the point where Stu was receiving hormone therapy, it could no longer be kept a secret. Issues arose among Stu's co-workers. One can only guess the number and types of issues, real or imagined, but we are going to focus on the first one.

One of the first issues to arise via a mechanics' union grievance was the question as to which locker room Stu/Sue should use, and when. It was a Catch-22 among the workforce. Neither the men nor the women were too keen on getting naked and showering next to him/her, particularly during the in-between stages of the process. And when does he officially become a she? A decision had to be made. What's yours?

Analysis

Believe it or not, this is actually a fairly easy one. The employer can defer this decision to the medical profession; specifically his/her own personal physician/psychologist team, as to when an employee uses which locker room while undergoing gender-reassignment. In other words, once Stu/Sue provides a letter of approval or recommendation from his/her doctor(s) that the procedure is advanced to the point where s/he can be considered a woman, then that is when the transfer should occur.

That's all well and good, but let's be practical here. It is still going to be a hard sell to Sue's co-workers. So, in order to ease the transition for everyone, it would also be advisable to inform co-workers as to the basis for the decision (i.e., legal and medical, not arbitrary) and some "sensitivity/diversity" training would be in order, as well. This is not easy for anyone: not for the employee undergoing the transformation, and not for his/her co-workers. There is no denying it; no pretending it will go away; no reason or advantage to side-step reality. It is what it is, and it needs to be out of the closet, just like Stu...or is it Sue?

And before you start crying the blues for Sue, understand that this was her decision, that she got the support of the company medical plan, and that part of her transition counseling includes dealing with all of the personal and emotional issues surrounding such a decision. It's your employees who are being blind-sided and for whom we must also show empathy and provide education.

This is the time to remind *all* workers of what constitutes sexual harassment and hostile environment and the consequences of it, as well as all the potential legal ramifications of working in today's "new normal" world of work. It doesn't have to revolve exclusively around the issue of Stu/Sue, nor should it, although most people will probably figure it out. Ideally, this type of training and awareness should have been taking place as standard procedure before a case like Stu's ever developed. If it hasn't, this is the time. But even if it has, this is a good time for a refresher course.

As a final aside, this might also be a good time to look at your locker room configurations, and if there is one large, common shower and dressing area, it might be worth considering partitions and more private accommodations. Regardless of the Stu/Sue scenario, most employees would rather dress, undress, and shower in private anyway, male or female. Wouldn't you?

A Boy Named Sue (Part 2)

OK, so now we've dealt with the locker room and sensitivity issues. But the saga continues. It's a year later, the gender-reassignment process is complete, and Sue is wearing dresses and make-up and using the ladies' locker room. Things have settled down somewhat, but now there is a job posting, and Sue bid on it. It's a promotion to a higher-grade position; one which s/he feels qualified to perform.

The job went to another bidder, a man (who has always been a man). Sue felt that she had been a victim of sex discrimination based on her new sex, and she filed suit against her employer. Is this possible? To be sued (no pun intended) by a female employee on the basis of being discriminated against as a woman, that the company subsidized to become a woman?

Analysis

Of course! You can sue for anything in this country! But can you believe that such a complicated case can actually be so easy to resolve? Yes, once again, the decision is an easy one. This case was tested beyond the Equal Employment Opportunity Commission (EEOC) level all the way to the courts, and the ruling has stood that, for purposes of enforcement of Title VII of the Civil Rights Act, employees are considered to be their sex at birth, regardless of gender-reassignment or any other effort at changing their real or perceived sex.

In other words, in the eyes of the EEOC, Stu is still Stu, and therefore cannot be protected by law as a woman. He can still sue for sex discrimination, but it would have to be as a man. Born a man, you can only be protected as a man. Because another man got the job, there was no basis (*prima facie*) for a discrimination case on the basis of sex.

As an aside, it is interesting to note that employers are increasingly adopting nondiscrimination policies pertaining to what are now being called GLBT (Gay, Lesbian, Bisexual, and Transgender) workers, who generally have had no legal protection from being fired if they express a nontraditional gender identity on the job. The Human Rights Campaign (HRC), a Washington, DC-based advocacy group, now publishes a Corporate Equality Index that rates companies on their policies regarding workers with nontraditional gender identities.

The Devil Made Me Do It!

Ben the Baptist was also a cop. Not a problem, until he was assigned to provide law-enforcement services at a casino. As a Baptist, Ben's belief was not only that he must not gamble, but also that he should do nothing that would help others to do so. Providing law enforcement services, in his mind, would be facilitating others' gambling, and thus he asked for a different assignment. The police department refused his request, so Ben felt he had no choice but to refuse to report for duty, and just stayed home. Does Ben have a religious right to refuse to work in a casino?

Analysis

No. Ben can be disciplined or even terminated. He is not being terminated or disciplined because of his beliefs. He is being terminated or disciplined for insubordination, for failure to report for duty. Allowing Ben or any law enforcement officer to pick and choose his or her assignments is an unreasonable expectation for the employer. It could even have an adverse impact on public safety, to which he and his fellow officers have a sworn duty.

Freedom *from* Religion?

Here's a new slant on freedom of religion....How about freedom "from" religion? Agnes was hired to be an executive housekeeper for a brand new hotel. One of her duties was to put a copy of the Gideon Bible in every room. During a meeting with her manager and the Gideons, they began to pray and read from the Bible. Agnes, who had no particular religious affiliation, was uncomfortable with the situation, and walked out of the meeting.

When her supervisor called her into his office to discuss this indiscretion, Agnes became quite belligerent and said that she is not required to participate in or be witness to a religious activity, particularly since she is not even a religious person. The conversation went downhill from there, which ultimately led her supervisor to fire her for insubordination. Is Agnes on terra firma or is she going straight to hell?

Analysis

Agnes' downfall is not her religion, but her lack of religion. She cannot claim the hotel discriminated against her because of her beliefs, because she doesn't have any! How can she force the hotel to accommodate her religious beliefs, particularly since the hotel cannot be expected to accommodate every contention that some aspect of a job violates some undefined religious belief?

Case dismissed! Now go straight to purgatory!

Minimum Coverage (Part 1)

Elizabeth, a divorced mother of two, was hired as a receptionist by a prestigious professional services firm, not only because she had the basic skills to do the job (keyboarding, filing, and telephone etiquette), but also because she possessed what used to be called "front office" appearance (before feminism defeated sexism in the world of employment law). Let's be honest. She was a hottie! OK? That doesn't make you a sexist!

Now that we have that established, the plot thickens. Being a divorced mom, Elizabeth worked two jobs to try and make ends meet and to save for her kids' college. In the old days, when it was still legal to hire someone for the front desk because they weren't ugly, holding a second job was called "moonlighting" because it was considered taboo and disloyal, and it was usually done at night. In this case, both might still be true. Why?

Because Elizabeth-by-day was "Betty Boop" by night. She was an exotic dancer. OK, she was a stripper. She wasn't performing in an off-Broadway version of *Cats*; she was twirling her tassels and bearing it all for tips. Enough said?

The grapevine at work was running rampant with stories and whispers intended for everyone to hear about "Betty's" other job. Eventually the human resources department felt it had no choice but to come out of denial, and to find a way to address the issue head on. Can they? Should they? And if so, how?

Analysis

From a purely legalistic, human resources point of view, it's none of their business. Unless, of course, her late working hours are causing Elizabeth to miss work, come in late, or not be attentive to her job. As you will learn, this will be one of the common answers to a lot of these cases, particularly those which involve an employee's "off-duty" behavior.

If it is not job-related and is not having a significant negative impact on the ability of others to perform or on the overall effectiveness of the organization, generally you should leave it alone. You don't have to love 'em, but in some cases you should just leave 'em alone.

Regarding the grapevine, about all that can be done, without exacerbating the situation, is to meet with all department heads and ask them to remind their employees in staff meetings that it is improper and unprofessional to engage in rumor-mongering and that what people do "off the clock" is generally none of their business. Any good manager should be in touch enough to know which of his or her employees are fertilizing the grapevine, but covering the subject in general as an agenda item at a staff meeting prevents finger-pointing and embarrassment, and is a good first step.

In order to avoid "highlighting" this case, it might be best to communicate the company position along with other periodically required policy announcements and reinforcements, such as sexual harassment policies, confidentiality agreements, conflicts of interest, and safety procedures. Otherwise, making a special issue out this situation could actually make it a bigger one since the grapevine is already well fertilized and receptive to even more manure.

As is the case with most "off-duty" behavior issues, it is next to impossible to create black-and-white policies to anticipate or to address all of them. To attempt to govern all questionable off-duty behavior would not only punish good people in the process, but it could also be viewed as "Big Brother-ism" and do more harm than good for the organization at large.

If, in fact, Betty Boop's job performance is suffering, you should address that, and that alone. You gain nothing and open the door to more problems by "assuming" her night job is to blame. Being a manager doesn't make you a psychic. There could be many causes of tardiness, absenteeism, poor performance, and the like. How do you know she doesn't have a substance abuse problem, or a child care problem, or some other issue?

The bottom line is, it really doesn't matter. Address the performance, give her a deadline for correction, and treat it like any other performance management challenge. As we discovered with Blue Suit Bob, by walking through the Behavioral Change Map, the rule of thumb is that the more one's off-duty behavior negatively affects workplace performance or the business as a whole, the more valid counseling, discipline, and even termination become as an option.

However, there are many federal and state laws that restrict the "at-will" doctrine of employment ("at-will" means you can be fired for any reason or no reason, as long as it's not illegal), and many employment experts believe it is morally wrong to fire people because you do not agree with their behavior or do not like what they do in their spare time.

Minimum Coverage (Part 2)

It gets better (or worse, depending on your perspective)! During a private counseling session with Elizabeth, she said, "I don't see why it is such a big deal that I perform at the club at night, especially since it is OK for the CEO to put ten dollar bills in my garter belt for personal lap dances!" *What*?

Yes, the CEO was a patron of the bootie club, and wasn't even aware that she was an employee of the firm. Not that it mattered, but now what? What response do you give "Betty" and what, if any, action should be taken regarding the CEO's extracurricular activities? Geeeze!

Analysis

Neither Betty nor the CEO are breaking the law (we assume it is a legal club in their jurisdiction), so technically it is no different than any other off-the-clock behavior that you may find abhorrent. You don't have to like it, but maybe they don't like some of the clubs you belong to either! And he is the boss!

Using the cost/benefit approach of the Behavioral Change Map (see page 140), an optional intervention that may be worthwhile would be to have either the top human resources executive or a close confidant of the CEO talk to him about his after-hours activities, particularly since he seems to be unaware that he is putting greenbacks into the G-string of one of his own employees.

It could even be couched in terms of the potential he has to compromise himself and the company since she is an employee of the company he leads. Putting a little fear of vulnerability in front of a CEO usually has some impact. You may even ask him what he would do if the media got hold of such a story. Again, even though he has the legal right to ogle boobies, he may come to the realization that this is not the type of image he may want to portray as the CEO. Ultimately the CEO sets the tone for everyone in the company, and if he is truly CEO material, he should be able to figure this out. If not, then you have bigger fish to fry.

If all else fails, a well-placed photo can be worth a thousand words! (Just kidding…maybe!)

Hoof-in-Mouth Hal

Hal is a very competent, talented techie. He is also a co-founder of Computergeeksolutions.com which is a company that essentially serves as a contract IT Department for small to mid-sized businesses that cannot afford to, nor justify, having their own IT Departments. His partner, Katie, is also a very competent technologist, and particularly good at sales and marketing calls. They have a staff of tech support personnel who answer customer support calls and go into the field when necessary.

CGS is in its third year of business, and Katie has been quite successful in lining up prospects and leads and "almost" closing deals. The problem is that Hal feels a need, and also a right, to accompany Katie on these sales calls, since he is a co-founder and partner of CGS. Unfortunately he is a one-stop-shop of political incorrectness and tactlessness.

Hal not only says the absolute wrong things at the wrong times to the wrong people, he doesn't even know when to shut up. Just when Katie has them warmed up to buy, Hal manages to stick his hoof in his mouth, and cannot seem to extricate it before the deal sours. Katie has them ready to ask, "Where do we sign?" until Hal gets them to say, "Don't call us, we'll call you!"

Whenever Katie tries to debrief a sales meeting with Hal, in an effort to get him to see the error of his ways, he just discounts everyone else who may be offended by his off-color, sexist, or political remarks as being uptight, too sensitive, or some other more disparaging label. It's never his problem! Remember low self-monitoring?

But it is Katie's problem because they are losing potential business, not to mention the impact it could eventually have on their reputation. It has reached a breaking point with Katie, but she is at a loss as to how to intervene and correct this situation, particularly since Hal is her "equal" business partner.

Analysis

There are actually several possible avenues available and/or necessary to deal with Hal. Before we explore them, however, let's go to the Behavioral Change Map again (Figure 2.2), and see where it takes us.

Although the flowchart tends to direct us to the conclusion that Hal's motivation is the issue, let's not be hasty. There is the possibility that he may lack some skills, so this case poses a caveat.

If Hal has never been diplomatic or politically correct, how do we know he can be? So, the first line of attack may be to convince him to take some type of interpersonal relations training (Dale Carnegie, et al.) and see if it sticks. That's one approach. But, knowing Hal, he may

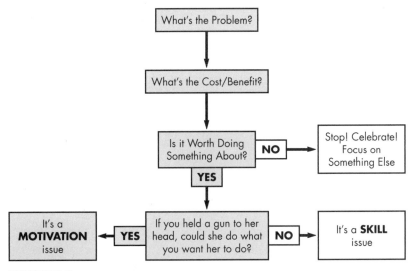

FIGURE 2.2

not be receptive to self-improvement, because, in his mind, it's everyone else who needs to change.

So, if that does not work, Katie may have to have a woman-to-man reality talk with Hal, to see if there might be a better place to use his *skills* to help grow the company, such as a more technical arena. But, since Hal may not be receptive to hearing this from Katie, an even better approach might be to solicit input from a board of directors, a small business advisory service, SCORE (Service Corps of Retired Executives), or some other non-biased, third-party business growth consultant or organization.

Regardless of who it is, they will tell them that one of the first rules of a successful business partnership is for the partners to have non-redundant skill sets. This is particularly necessary when you are lean staffed, because you do not have the luxury of allowing two people to do the same thing at the same time (i.e., double team sales calls), unless each brings enough of a unique value to the table. That is not the case here. Hal adds nothing to the situation. Just don't tell him that.

Finally, if Hal does not respond to interpersonal effectiveness training (i.e., it is not a skill issue), and Katie and the consultants cannot "motivate" him to bow out of the sales side of the business, perhaps a trial period of Katie and Hal going on separate sales calls (use productivity as an ego-saving ploy) for a period of time to see who has the best success might convince Hal of the virtues of change. After all, as a co-founder, Hal has to be motivated by business growth, so if he can see that his own wallet will be fatter if he applies himself where he is most valuable, the proof will be in the pudding!

This may be a good time to look at the "AIM" Venn Diagram in Chapter 4, because if you drill down as to why Hal may be so flippant about sales, it may be because deep down he knows he is not very good at it or just doesn't like it. But with his ego and defensiveness, it is easier to just discount it to save face. Few of us love to do something that we cannot do well, particularly on a regular basis. It is particularly troubling if Hal has neither the *A*bility nor the *I*nterest.

Bottom line: You will be doing Hal a favor by finding a graceful way for him to bow out of the sales call process. Tap his real abilities and interests such as analyses, written proposals, projections, cost-benefit analyses, etc., and find a way to weave those into an asset to the sales process so he still feels like a contributor, his ego is protected, and both of you can be successful.

If all of these approaches fail, Katie should just buy him out!

Note

The relationship between the Behavioral Change Map and the AIM Diagram: the Behavioral Change Map forces you to make a distinction between one's "skills" and one's "motivation." They either can't do it, or don't want to do it. The AIM diagram drives the point home that without "abilities" (i.e., skills) and "interest" (motivation) one's long-term success is limited. See the correlation?

If You Want the Job Done Right!

Rodney was a creative genius, a budding inventor, and an entrepreneur. He spent several years on his own, on a product that he developed and had patented, and that appeared to hold the promise of fame and fortune. He also spent those years as a loner, by choice. In spite of several highly successful businessmen's offers of support, both financial and professional, Rodney just couldn't share his baby with anyone. He not only feared that someone might steal his secret, but also believed that no one could do things as well as he. He was wrong.

After years of financial ruin, he never really gave up on his invention. That could never happen. But reality finally required that he go back to work for a company. And Rodney found what appeared to be the perfect compromise: a technology development company that prided itself on repeated *successful* new product introductions to the market. Innovation, capital, and implementation all under one roof!

Being highly self-motivated, Rodney did quite well at first, working diligently on a promising new proprietary chemical compound. He not only met his new employer's deadlines and budget, but did so with aplomb. So what's the problem? The problem is that Rodney refused to let anyone else in the innovation chain of command participate in any of it, including the later stages of development—prototypes, packaging, market research, etc. It didn't matter that he had no proven expertise or even any accountability for these responsibilities.

Rodney's "close to the vest" mentality that sank him as an entrepreneur was haunting him still. Once again, he was trapped in the mindset that no one but he was as qualified or capable of taking a project from beginning to end. But this time, it wasn't his call.

But how does an employer capitalize on Rodney's innovative brilliance without driving him away? How do we keep control of the process without losing Rodney in the process?

Analysis

Since Rodney is already on the payroll, and you already know he has value, we need to find a way to tap his talent without stifling his motivation. The first and most effective way (see Behavioral Change Map in Chapter 4) is to manage the consequences; in this case, money (compensation, bonuses, and incentives)!

It may be too late to restructure his base salary (i.e., to reduce it), so we need to find a way to dangle a win-win carrot in front of him, something that we can afford if he meets the objectives, such as a bonus for getting the new product to market by a certain date, or cooperating with certain other key members of the team, based on feedback reports and tangible, indisputable measures. This way, he will have no choice but to "let go" and to learn that he is not the only one with a brain and valuable talent.

Simultaneous to this strategy, you should put Rodney through a psychological assessment process. Let's call it personal development. It's less threatening. You will learn what you already know, that he is a creator, not an implementer, *but he needs to learn it too*! He also needs to learn how others can actually help him succeed. Right now, Rodney would rather fail than admit that he cannot do it all.

Ideally, this issue should have been nipped in the bud, at the point of hire. Not only because it is common for creative and innovative geniuses to also be prima donnas, but also because there are ways to predict and even prevent these behaviors, through psychological testing and profiling. Granted, it may not change Rodney (or anyone like him), but it does afford a reality check up front as to what to expect, and allows you to structure the job and its compensation (consequences) to drive the appropriate behaviors.

For example, some people are creative thinkers like Rodney, while others' strengths may lie in the area of development or advancement of an idea, taking an idea and turning the concept into a reality, while others are implementers, taking it to the market and selling it, and so forth.

Very, very few people, even geniuses, can excel at all of these functions (see AIM to Be Weird, Chapter 4) because they may lack either the ability or the interest to some degree, thus making someone else more qualified.

Once your team recognizes this reality, they can then see the value, both to them and to the organization, of how a true innovation team can and should be formed. With proper assessment and placement, you can create a truly whole-brained team in which no one feels threatened, but all feel enlightened.

Al Naturale

All in favor of diversity, say Aye! All in favor of tolerance, say Aye! All in favor of body odor, say…

Yes, Technerd Industries, Inc. was a company that exemplified the concept of diversity and tolerance. They hired engineers, scientists, and every other skilled trade from around the globe. They even facilitated and subsidized immigrants' efforts at gaining citizenship in order to stay in the U.S. and work for their company. They valued talent, period! Bring us your huddled masses! And it worked. They hired the best and the brightest, and had fewer recruitment challenges than most of their competitors. When you worked at Technerd, you knew that diversity and tolerance of others were the hallmarks of their culture.

But, there was a limit, at least in the eyes (and noses) of the "sweet smelling" camp. It was just expected that everyone would come to work in the morning smelling fresh or not smelling at all. But, it became common knowledge that a detour was necessary when traveling the halls and cubicles of Technerd if you did not want to experience the sensory sensation of Mr. Al Naturale. Bottom line: He had extreme body odor, and no amount of incense or air freshener could cover it up. That would be like trying to spray perfume on a piece of poop.

Finally, a group of standard-smelling serfs stormed the Human Resources office to file a formal complaint. They made it clear that it was not only offensive, but also a deterrent to their productivity and morale. One comment made was, "What ever happened to majority rule? Al is in a distinct minority, and not only in the legal sense of the word. Something has to be done!"

What would you do?

Analysis (Part 1)

Every organization should seek diversity. Diversity means different points of view, and different points of view mean more ideas and greater potential for creativity. But diversity has limits. Those limits include not having to put up with someone's body odor, which makes it difficult to concentrate and work effectively.

Just as an employer has the right to set minimum typing speeds for typists, it has the right to decide whether its workplace is smoke-free or odor-free. Here Al's co-workers found it difficult to maintain productivity and morale. Why? He smells bad! This has nothing to do with disliking how someone "different" looks or acts. Al's smells weren't just different. They were offensive, and Technerd has a right to have him shape up or ship out.

Having to tell an employee that his body odor offends others is not a pleasant task, but ignoring the problem is only going to create more problems down the road with his co-workers. Before meeting with Al, it would be prudent to investigate the allegations, assuming you have never been downwind of him yet, to confirm that the complaints are legitimate.

Upon confirmation of the stench, schedule a private meeting with Al to address the issue. Be sensitive, but direct. Treat it as you would any other job-related issue, because it is. If the opportunity presents itself, suggest measures for correcting the problem, like bathing daily and wearing deodorant.

One caution, however: Do not suggest possible medical causes for body odor because doing so could lead to implications related to the

Americans with Disabilities Act (ADA). If Al volunteers such information, i.e., that the condition is medically related, ask for a physician's certification to determine if, in fact, he does have an ADA-protected disability. If so, then you must determine if a reasonable accommodation is feasible. For more information on ways to accommodate employees with medically related body odor, see the web site of the Job Accommodation Network, a service of the U.S. Department of Labor's Office of Disability Employment Policy at *www.jan.wvu.edu*. The page on body odor is at *www.jan.wvu.edu/soar/other/bodyodor.html*.

Al Naturale (Part 2)

Upon counseling Al, his supervisor discovered that Al's culture and religion do not believe in the use of perfumes or other artificial substances on their bodies. Is Al's right to smell protected by law, as a religious freedom or right to free expression?

Analysis (Part 2)

It may sound un-American, but legally speaking, if Al works for a private employer, he has no right to freedom of expression in the workplace. Private means not part of the federal, state, or local government system. Federal and state constitutions protect folks from *government* abuse. Al has no constitutional rights, such as freedom of speech or expression, subject to protection from a private employer.

But claiming religious preference and religious discrimination makes the situation more interesting. Hasidic Jews, as an example, are an extremely orthodox branch of the Jewish faith. As a matter of religion, they use no soaps or perfumes. On a hot summer day in a New York subway, dressed in dark, heavy clothing, they can get a bit "ripe." But they can do that, free of discrimination, because the transit system ordinarily is owned or authorized by a local government, and travelers have constitutional rights to freedom of religion and expression.

But a private employer like Technerd is different. It probably is subject to Title VII of the Civil Rights Act, state, and local laws which forbid religious discrimination. Put another way, Technerd cannot treat people adversely because of their religion and must reasonably accommodate people's religious convictions.

But what if an employer has a job-related reason for something that unintentionally impacts a person's religious convictions adversely, or someone's religious observance causes hardship to the employer? The law permits such "discrimination." In Al's case the hardship to Technerd's business is evident. His smells make it difficult for employees to concentrate at work. If Technerd cannot force or persuade Al to eliminate or control his odor, employees will not be able to work effectively and otherwise efficiently. That would hurt the business, and that permits Technerd, within reason, to clamp down on Al and his smells.

But what if Al works alone in his own office and a ventilating system could make virtually all of his smells disappear? What if Al works strictly on a computer with no human contact, customer or employee? In either situation, and if Al's smells are driven by religious belief, the employer may not suffer a sufficient hardship to "de-skunk" him. In that situation, or in a disability case (Al may smell because he has some disease), Technerd should engage in a dialogue with him to learn about his smells, their root, the detrimental effect they are having on the business, and balancing odor and business.

Why? To explore and hopefully find a way to eliminate or drastically reduce the problem with the least effort, cost, and infringement on Al. If Technerd does this, it is on a far firmer legal footing, regardless of its final decision.

Chatty Cathy

Cathy is an accomplished creative writer. She works in a cubicle. So do her neighboring co-workers. Unfortunately for them, Cathy's way of processing concepts is to think out loud. She talks to herself, all day, almost all the time. Whether it's just a nervous habit, or her way of thinking and problem solving, no one really cares. All they know is that it is annoying and distracting.

After a while, her co-workers started to listen more closely to see if they could eavesdrop on her self-talk and see if they could get her into trouble for something. However, all they could hear was her talking her way through various projects, brainstorming alternative creative commercials, rehearsing her next phone conversation, and other non-descript but job-related banter.

But that didn't make it any less irritating. The troops managed to get their collective bowels into an uproar, and eventually Nellie, who works in one of the adjacent cubicles, was nominated to go to her boss to see if he could put a muzzle on Cathy. She claimed that it was an infringement on their personal peace and space, and that it was just weird, and that she and her fellow eavesdroppers were sick of it.

Should Cathy be muzzled?

Analysis

This has to be a common phenomenon in today's open office environments. But why should Cathy's self-talk be any more distracting than if she were on the phone all day? The bottom line is that Cathy's co-workers are bothered more by her weirdness than by her talking. Unless Cathy is screaming, or spewing obscenities, or truly creating a hostile work environment, it's no one's business that she has a weird habit of talking to herself. Not to mention the fact that she has a successful track record of idea development, thoroughness, and other performance indices that prove that her method works for her.

There is a solution, however, for anyone working in such an environment. It's called white noise. Many companies, unbeknownst to anyone, pipe in a constant shhhhhhh sound that is amazingly effective at canceling out or covering up conversation. It is more for privacy purposes than anything else, but it does work. In fact, in my early days in labor relations, and before the technology of white noise existed, we would caucus in the bathroom of our hotel room next to a running shower in case the room was bugged. Low-tech white noise! Same principle.

Assuming Cathy's company does not want to invest in white noise, Nellie and her nosy friends can buy their own personal noise cancellation headsets, which do the same thing, but even better. They aren't for playing music, unless you want them to, but they do cancel out extraneous noise. Some people use them on airplanes so they can sleep while their noisy fellow passengers hoot and holler.

There are plenty of personal solutions that Nellie and friends can pursue such as mini-waterfalls, low music, etc. without having to embarrass or inconvenience Cathy, who is harming no one. Otherwise, tell Nellie and her friends to pay more attention to what's going on inside their own cubicles and maybe they won't be so easily distracted.

Walking Art

Art is a Gen "Y" individualist whose hobby is to "personalize" his body. He has a bolt through his nose, a stud in his tongue, rings through his eyebrows and tattoos in all the right (or wrong) places. Art thinks of himself as, well…exactly that… living, walking "art."

The problem is that Art is a front line service worker in an assisted living facility for senior citizens, and his appearance scares the bejeepers out of these poor folks. One man almost had a heart attack when Art walked into his room one night to clean his bathroom. Residents walk on the opposite sides of the hallways when Art approaches. It has become a recurring topic of conversation in the dining room, and elsewhere in the community among the residents.

Art claims that his "body art" falls into his right to personal freedom of expression, and that he has a lifestyle outside of work that respects and even admires his sense of style, and that people just need to lighten up, be more open minded, and get used to the "diversity" of today's generation. After all, we always talk about tolerance and acceptance of diversity, so why should he be "discriminated" against? Shouldn't people just learn to adapt?

Analysis

NOPE! Self-inflicted diversity is not a protected class. Art wasn't born with a bolt in his nose, or a naked lady on his forearm, so just give up on the diversity angle. Art can express himself as painfully as he wishes when he is off the clock, but given the nature of the customer and the business, it is no different than requiring the wearing of hair nets in the kitchen.

After all, some organizations legitimately and legally prohibit beards for those who may have to wear respirators in an emergency. Other companies prohibit the use of foul language to prevent creating a hostile work environment for others. Art can express himself somewhere else.

A reasonable solution may be to have Art remove his hardware and to cover up his tattoos with long sleeves and pants to whatever extent is possible while on duty. He is not impressing senior citizens with his personal expression, and he is not being denied his so-called right to express himself in the outside world.

Ultimately, if he cannot put a lid on his self-expression, your decision becomes one of placement elsewhere, like in the kitchen or some other less visible position, if he is worth keeping at all. It is job-related, period!

Somebody's Got to Do It!

Hardcore Software, Inc. is a leader in servicing a multitude of clients in the X-rated, adult e-commerce and web-based entertainment industry with everything from web design, merchant account processing systems, video streaming, and even content development. In other words, they serve the purveyors of Internet porn.

In the process of providing these services, it is an inescapable reality that employees are subjected to graphic sexual images and activities, and, as in any service-related company, they are also expected to have positive interactions and to even schmooze with client representatives on occasion.

Mary, a junior staff member, has been with HSI for six months, and has managed to avoid all contact with clients. She conveniently makes herself unavailable for company/client activities such as trade shows, sales meetings, socials, and other gatherings, by always having a "personal" excuse like a family emergency, doctor's appointment, spontaneous vacation plans, personal business, etc.

Her opinion of the clients and the industry are well known, as she continually makes pejorative comments to her co-workers about them both, with utter disgust. But the job pays well, it meets her needs geographically, and offers her the flexible work schedule she needs. So, she has decided to tolerate the "other" issues.

Mary's savvy at being invisible around the client and at never being available for other business development activities has started to rub her co-workers the wrong way. It has also come to a head with her supervisor, who feels these roles are a necessary and required part of the job.

Upon meeting with Mary about these issues, Mary said that she was hired to do a specific job, and that she does that job well. To participate in these extra-curricular activities with people she considers lewd and lascivious goes against her values and her religious upbringing and that if she is forced to do so, she will file a charge of sexual harassment by reason of hostile work environment.[1]

---

1. There are two bases for filing sexual harassment charges: 1) Quid Pro Quo: occurs when an employer or supervisor links specific employment outcomes to the individual's granting sexual favors, i.e., sleep with me and you'll get that promotion, and 2) Hostile Environment: occurs when sexual harassment has the effect of reasonably interfering with employee work performance or psychological well-being, or when intimidating or offensive working conditions are created.

Analysis

If, in fact, networking and schmoozing are an integral part of Mary's job, this issue can be dealt with as purely a performance issue, which is the preferable route for Hardcore Software. Ideally, this would have been part of her original job description and even part of any new employee's orientation program.

An effective new employee orientation program should be about more than just how to fill out benefit forms or where the restrooms and cafeteria are located. Orientation programs should be used to instill values: specifically, company values. And the values of a company like HSI are not hard to understand. Difficult to respect, maybe, but not hard to understand.

And long before an employee is hired, at any company, but especially one like HSI, it is critical that employment candidates be given something called a "Realistic Job Preview," or RJP. Too many companies see recruitment as more of a sales pitch and only tell people the good stuff, rather than as an opportunity and an obligation to have both parties assess whether they will be a fit for each other.

An RJP gives candidates the good stuff, but also makes sure they are aware of the potential downsides of working at a particular company. Whether it is extensive travel, difficult customers, odd hours, challenging conditions, or whatever, it does neither party any good to hide the bad and the ugly parts of working there only to have them revealed after they are hired. For Hardcore Software Inc., it is particularly important to be sure that candidates understand the nature of their clientele, their products, services, and expectations.

In extreme cases, some employers have even been granted a special exception, called a BFOQ (bona fide occupational qualification), which actually allows them to discriminate on otherwise illegal bases and exempts them from potential employment discrimination claims.

For example, a man might not be able to sue a lingerie catalogue for refusing to hire him as a model, even though it was obviously based upon his sex. Their customers do not want to see a guy's marble bag wrapped in silk. Or, a black cosmetics company might discriminate against a Caucasian to demonstrate their line of products, even though it is clearly discrimination on the basis on race.

Additionally, there have been cases (*Ocheltree v. Scollon Productions, Inc.*, 4th Cir., No. 01-1648) in which the courts have ruled against a female employee who complained of offensive sexual conduct and language by male co-workers, holding that sexually explicit jokes and language directed at and offensive to *both* genders cannot constitute discrimination because of sex. An employee is discriminated against "because of sex" only if the conduct would not have occurred but for the employee's gender, the court held.

Although anyone can sue anyone for anything in this country, unless there was some targeted activity toward Mary causing her emotional distress of a sexual nature, she would be hard pressed to be able to make a claim of hostile work environment. And, to reaffirm, if the nature of her job requires socializing and interacting with clients, HSI would be perfectly within its rights to counsel her based upon not meeting the performance expectations of the job.

What's It to Ya?

Cliques are nothing new. They form at school; they form at work; they even form at church. But one clique in particular seems to trouble everyone who isn't in it. Every day at lunchtime, Stan and a handful of employees gather at one table and pretty much shun everyone else. They seem to always be planning something together for evenings, weekends, etc. And they seem to have a real attitude about it.

So what? Others are on bowling leagues together; they go to sporting events, picnics, and all sorts of other "group" activities. Why so much fuss about this clique? Just because they are all white men with shaved heads, risqué tattoos, muscle shirts with swastikas, and narrow views on the roles of minorities and other protected classes in society?

Exactly! They were Ku Klux Klan, white supremacist skinheads! Now what?

Analysis

The employer here is almost certainly subject to federal, state, and/or local laws forbidding workplace discrimination, including, in particular, prohibiting racial, national origin, and religious workplace discrimination. That means that an employer has a duty to keep its workplace free of discrimination by everyone, not just its supervisors, but also its employees, vendors, and customers.

It is illegal and also unwise (and loony!) for an employer subject to these laws to allow an organization like this one to advocate white supremacy at the workplace. Our "equal employment" employer therefore needs to clamp down on this clique, by written policy and warnings of discharge. In no uncertain terms, our EEO employer has to make absolutely clear to this klan that it has no right, in the workplace, to act upon or even voice any deep-seated feelings that run contrary to our equal employment laws. *If* they want to stay employed!

To the extent any of these supremacist skinheads manifest anti-race, anti-national origin, or anti-religious actions or words ever again, we can say "sayonara" to them, once and for all. Saying goodbye in Japanese would be an ironic send-off to let everyone and anyone know that diversity is *good* and for them to make themselves "diverse" by leaving the workplace, never to return.

But what of their freedom of association, expression, or speech? As mentioned earlier (see Al Naturale), there are no such animals if our equal opportunity employer is a private (i.e., non-government) company. But even if it is a public employer, employees making up the KKK clique have no *unlimited* right of association, expression, or speech, where it will or can cause dissension, confusion, or outright violence in the workplace. That is the reason why no one, for instance, has a right to yell "Fire!" in a crowded movie theatre because the ensuing panic could kill or injure people.

Abused and Confused

Suzie was the receptionist at a major financial services firm. She greeted folks as they came into the main office, managed the switchboard, and did some filing and typing in between. Her attendance was good, her skills were fine and she was well liked by everyone. But apparently things weren't going so well for Suzie at home. She would come to work wearing long sleeves in the middle of summer, heavier make-up than usual, and even tinted glasses on occasion. She was even heard crying in the ladies room when she thought no one was around.

Eventually the grapevine was quite fertilized, and there was no avoiding the issue any longer. It was obvious, even to customers and other outsiders who came to visit, that Suzie was being abused by someone. So, her supervisor asked Human Resources for assistance. What could they do to help Suzie without prying into her personal life? Do they have a right to talk with her about it? Her job performance continues to be fine, but it is causing tension and distraction among employees and particularly with customers, vendors, and others with whom the firm does business.

Analysis

Let's go back to the Behavioral Change Map one more time (Figure 2.3).

In this case, we don't need to waste a lot of time defining the problem or doing a cost/benefit analysis or even belaboring whether this is worth doing something about. One's life and limb may be at stake here, not to mention the negative impact this has on customers, clients, and co-workers.

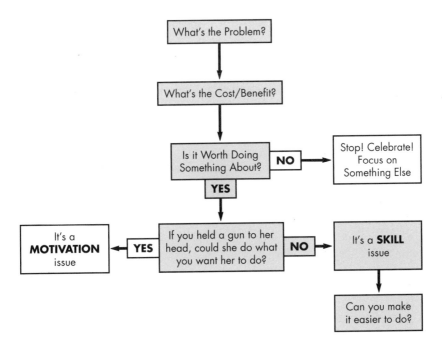

FIGURE 2.3

And believe it or not, many individuals in this situation are completely blinded by it, and cannot even see any options for dealing with it, so it's certainly not a motivation issue. So, if it's a skill issue, the next question is, "Can you make it easier for her to do?" And the answer is "Yes."

Analysis (Part 1)

Human Resources suggested referring Suzie to the Employee Assistance Program (EAP), a confidential, third party provider of counseling and referral services, and tried to avoid getting into the specifics of her personal life. They decided that it would be okay to let her know that they were concerned about her well-being, but they could not force her into counseling or to seek legal counsel.

There was no denying that she was coming to work bruised and battered, so whether she wants to admit to the cause or not is up to her.

From a human resources perspective, since her job skills were not lacking, and her attendance was not suffering, there was no basis for "performance counseling." So Human Resources, along with her immediate supervisor, agreed to sit down with Suzie and make her aware of the obvious, and to suggest she contact the Employee Assistance Program provider.

Abused and Confused (Part 2)

When Suzie's supervisor and HR sat down with her to make her aware of the EAP, she just clammed up. She refused to acknowledge that there was any problem at all, and even suggested that her bruises were due to a fall and then from some extra-curricular sports activities. When confronted about her crying in the ladies room, she said that she has always had mood swings, that maybe it's some hormonal thing.

It was obvious that Suzie was in total denial and was probably afraid to reveal the true nature of her situation and cause of her injuries. HR and her supervisor were also in no position to insist upon any further action at this time.

As might be expected, Suzie's situation did not improve. In fact, things only got worse. It got so bad that her supervisor actually pulled her off the job one morning when she was obviously injured to tell her that she had to deal with whatever the issue is because it was beginning to detract from her effectiveness on the job, with her co-workers and with the public. In this regard, and to this degree, it *is* job-related and not just personal any more.

She finally confessed that her boyfriend was the jealous, possessive type and that he was always accusing her of all kinds of suspicious activity, and that no matter what she said or did it always ended the same way. She would deny it but then he would call her a liar, blow up, and then beat her up. She said that he would always apologize later and promise that it would never happen again, but eventually it always did.

To complicate matters even further, she was now in fear for her life. She said that she could not go to the Employee Assistance Program because her boyfriend would never permit her "airing their dirty laundry" and that this would make him look bad, and only make matters even worse for her and her daughter. He made it quite clear that if she ever breathed a word of their domestic situation to anyone that she and her daughter would regret it, so she is between a rock and a hard place.

Analysis (Part 2)

Now that Suzie has confirmed her situation with her employer, they and/or the Employee Assistance Program (EAP) personnel are in a position to give her appropriate counsel. Ideally, it should come from the EAP to keep it confidential, and because that is what they are paid and trained to do.

Although it may not happen, the logical next step is to get Suzie to separate herself from this guy, and to get a restraining order against him. Each year, over a million employees become victims of violent crime at work, according to the U.S. Department of Justice. When violence from domestic partners threatens to spill over into the workplace, employers should use every tool available to protect themselves and their employees. It's no longer personal; it's their business!

One of these tools is a court restraining order barring an aggressor from the workplace. Although we see them violated time and time again in the news, restraining orders are still one of the only legal and necessary tools available in the fight against abuse, whether at home or at work.

Restraining orders are creatures of state law, and as such, vary widely from one state to another on a variety of issues. Therefore, it is best to seek specific advice from an expert in employment law in your state. And, once again, this should be something that your EAP should be able to orchestrate.

As a final note, the employer may want to take other general actions to protect themselves and their workers on an ongoing basis, not just for this type of situation, but to adapt to the unfortunate nature of today's society. Such measures might include installing surveillance cameras in public places, controlling workplace access, making sure all employees are aware of their EAP and how to use it, posting and/or distributing domestic violence and rape hotline numbers, etc. Education can be one of the best forms of prevention and correction.

Got Milk?

Lacy is a new mother. She returned to work as soon as her medical leave for pregnancy expired. Although she is not a "stay-at-home" mother advocate, she is a devotee of breast-feeding. Dilemma? How can she nurse her baby, when her breasts are at work, and her baby is across town at the day care center? Simple! Use a breast pump at work to stockpile her milk to deliver to the day care center the next day.

Sounds simple enough, but Lacy's need (desire?) to lactate didn't always coincide with her scheduled break times or lunch time. So, she just whipped those puppies out and pumped her product whenever and wherever the mood (or pressure) hit her. Yuck! Excuse me, but I'm a guy, and I don't even want to look at that at work!

When people treated her behavior like a car wreck (looking, but not looking), and some even sighed in disgust or left the area, Lacy's militant motherness was also exposed, along with her breasts. She would, in no uncertain terms, cast dispersions upon those who could be so insensitive toward a mother's desire to breast-feed, or who were turned off by such a beautiful and natural event of nature.

Again, excuse me, but there are plenty of "acts of nature" that we all experience, many of which are intended to be out of range of others' senses and sensibilities. (Does the bathroom come to mind here?) So what is an employer to do? Does Lacy's need translate into a right?

Analysis

No! OK, next question? All right, so it may not be so simple and straightforward as that. Otherwise, why put it in the book, right? Actually it depends on the state. As of this writing, laws in California (surprise?), Connecticut, Hawaii, Illinois, Minnesota, and Tennessee require employers to provide an appropriate workplace location—other than a restroom—where nursing mothers can "express" milk. Other states, like Texas and Washington, have programs designed to encourage employers to be "infant-friendly."

Otherwise, it's a business judgment call. Except where proscribed by law, there is no reason why an employer cannot counsel an employee like Lacy to be more discreet about when and where she lactates. Granted, you may want to be a little more flexible about enforcing scheduled break times, but you do not have to provide more off-duty time for a nursing mother any more than you do for people who have to step outside to have a nicotine fix. It's not the "when" that is as business driven as the "how much" or the "where."

For the latest state laws covering this subject, go to *www.lalecheleague.org/LawBills.html*. The La Leche League is obviously pro-breast-feeding, and even cites evidence that working mothers who breast-feed have lower absenteeism rates than those who bottle-feed their babies. Go figure.

Quid Pro Quo *Pro* (AKA Tit for Tat)

As was defined in "Somebody's Got To Do It!" there are two forms of sexual harassment (see footnote on page 50). That particular case had to do with hostile environment. This one has to do with quid pro quo, but with a twist, of course!

Loretta was Executive Vice President of Clean & Pure, the largest division of a high-end cosmetics corporation. There were quite a few female executives in this company who had worked their way up the ladder the old fashioned way—through hard work—and managed to break through the glass ceiling. This was one company that recognized and rewarded performance, regardless of sex.

Lou started out as a sales representative in the field, calling on department store buyers. He reported to Jim, a Regional Sales Manager. Ultimately, Jim reported to Loretta, but there were several layers of management between them.

Loretta and Lou met at the company's annual sales conference in Las Vegas, and really hit it off. In fact, they hit it off in the elevator, in the lounge, and eventually in Loretta's executive suite. In the afterglow of the evening, they both realized what they had done (yeah, right!), and Lou said that he was sorry for the indiscretion and that it would end there.

Loretta had other ideas. She told Lou that she doesn't just hit and run, and that if he wasn't interested in continuing the tryst, that he truly did have poor judgment, and that she questioned his future potential at Clean & Pure. Lou was shocked, but decided that since he was in Las Vegas, he needed to know when to hold 'em and when to fold 'em. So, he called her hand!

"What's in it for me, Loretta? I have nothing to gain here but a roll in the hay. Not that it wasn't enjoyable, but you are threatening my future career if I don't sleep with you. So, what if I do?" said Lou.

"Lou, you know that Jim, your boss, is not going to be in that position forever. Just think about it. Who do you think has the final say about such promotions and transfers? You can have your cake and eat it too! Don't be stupid," said Loretta.

And so it went. Ordinarily this would be a clear case of quid pro quo, and a sexual discrimination charge would be pending. But not this time. Lou went for it, hook, line, and sinker. He became Regional Sales Manager within a year, then moved into Corporate Headquarters where he could really make his mark, both personally and professionally. And he did. Raises, promotions, cushy projects, and favored assignments came his way. Lou was the fat rich kid in the candy store.

The only problem was that everyone knew what was going on, including those who did not receive the promotions, assignments, and other "fringe benefits" of sleeping with the boss. Resentment turned to pent-up anger because it seemed futile to do or say anything about it. After all, Loretta's character is pretty well established by now, so it's doubtful she would just suddenly "see the light" and repent! What to do! What to do!

Analysis

Well, the first question is "who cares?" Not to imply that this isn't totally inappropriate, unfair, and a gross abuse of power, but seriously, what action is taken next depends literally on who cares. In other words, is it Lou's former peers, or is it Loretta's boss? Position power does matter in how a case like this is initiated. Let's face it: neither Loretta nor Lou are going to initiate it!

Assuming it is someone above Loretta (on the organizational chart, that is) who is concerned, a rather standard internal investigation could be initiated in which the parties are interviewed separately, corroboration is sought, evidence is obtained, and ultimatums are presented. Pretty clear cut. Well, as clear cut as a sexual harassment investigation can be, that is. Any employment lawyer or consultant worth his or her salt can walk them through that one.

But, what if the higher ups have no clue, or are in denial? And what if the complaints are coming from those whom Lou slept over (instead of stepped over) on his way to the top? Well, as you are probably starting to realize by now, there are multiple possibilities and scenarios.

The worst-case scenario would be a complaint being lodged by someone who felt he or she was denied a promotion or other employment opportunity due substantially to the quid pro quo relationship between Lou and Loretta. First, one must demonstrate that 1) an opportunity existed in which the aggrieved party was eligible and qualified, 2) that Lou was awarded the opportunity, and 3) that he was awarded the opportunity due to the quid pro quo relationship. That's called a *prima facie* case.

Long before it gets to the point of litigation, however, it is critical that the employer have a clearly communicated process for complaints such as this to be filed and given due process, and that a full, impartial, confidential investigation be conducted promptly. Ideally, this process should be spearheaded by someone in a human resources or legal capacity to better ensure objectivity and confidentiality. Again, evidence is collected and the parties are interviewed.

Whether Lou and/or Loretta admit to their sins or not is a consideration, but if the evidence clearly indicates that the case has merit, the liability for the employer is the same. This type of case could be resolved internally, or may require litigation, depending upon 1) the actions taken to punish the offenders and 2) the acceptance of the terms by the aggrieved party or parties.

Sanctions could run anywhere from a serious warning with orders to cease and desist from future trysts and special favors, all the way to termination and corrective action. It is at this point that legal counsel should determine the proper intervention based upon the specifics and seriousness of the case.

If, in fact, the worst-case scenario is true, then the employer might be justified in terminating the employment of both Lou and Loretta. Loretta's role and culpability as victimizer and power abuser is clear. But even though Lou may appear to have been a victim of Loretta, he continued to use the situation to his personal gain and could have disclosed the impropriety of Loretta's quid pro quo actions through the same due process as his colleagues did to ultimately bring it to the attention of the company.

In any event, the message must be clear that such behavior will not be tolerated and that the company's sexual harassment policies and procedures are effective at both weeding out and dealing with such situations.

When Perception Ain't Reality

It is said that perception is reality. In other words, if you believe something is true, you will behave as if it is. This is true! But when it causes upheaval and expense, and the perception is based on a falsehood, it may be time for a reality check.

Lizzie was working as an assembly-line worker in a manufacturing plant, when Marcus, a co-worker next to her, cut his hand, resulting in some of his blood spattering onto her hand. Unfortunately, Lizzie was of the opinion that Marcus was gay, based upon his mannerisms, his circle of friends, etc. As a result, she panicked, made a great scene, and appropriately washed the blood off and found the first-aid kit and applied antiseptic immediately.

But it didn't end there. In addition to creating a scene on the job, she insisted that the company pay for an HIV test for her, which they did. It came back negative. But that wasn't good enough for Lizzie. She just couldn't get it out of her head that she was in great danger of contracting AIDS, and even though subsequent tests continued to confirm that she was HIV-negative, she was just too traumatized to work. Not surprisingly, Lizzie found a doctor to diagnose her with post-traumatic stress disorder, which she used as a basis to apply for Workers' Compensation. Should she be entitled to it?

Analysis

Ordinarily, this could be a jump ball, dependent upon the jurisdiction in which the worker applied for his or her workers' compensation, the mood and politics of the hearing officer, or any of a number of other uncontrollable variables in the world of government benefits.

In fact, Lizzie was actually awarded benefits, based upon her medical diagnosis of post-traumatic stress disorder. However, the company appealed the decision, which went all the way to a state level Supreme Court, which reversed the decision to award benefits because her claim was based upon a "fear" of exposure as opposed to "actual" exposure through a medically recognized means of transmission.

The learning point here is that employers, particularly those where bodily fluids may be involved (healthcare, etc.), should educate their employees about the known ways in which HIV and any other diseases may (or may not) be transmitted. Education is the best way to prevent unfounded fears based upon rumor, innuendo, or other misguided assumptions.

Additionally, there are regulations promulgated by the Occupational Safety and Health Administration (OSHA) that include detailed guidelines related to blood-borne pathogens which were created to minimize the potential for transmission of HIV and other blood-borne diseases. Adherence to these guidelines will reduce employees' fears and ability to claim "actual" exposure.

Ticks & Twitches

Terry is a rather introverted but very effective employee, and whenever he gets in a group setting, he seems to get nervous and starts making weird faces and noises. His co-workers have come to expect it, and even have a good laugh about it behind his back. He has a number of body ticks and twitches that seem to be out of his control.

Whether Terry is aware of how he looks and sounds is anyone's guess, but it is becoming more of an issue now that he has to meet with clients. He is the only one who really understands the intricacies of their technology and who can translate it in such a way that clients can see the value of expanding its applications. He is a rare talent, but also a strange bird.

The last time they were meeting with a client in the conference room, Terry got one of his looks of constipation and consternation, and the client thought he was mad about something. Red faces abounded, and what used to be just an inside joke was becoming an embarrassment. How can we solve this problem without destroying Terry's self-esteem and particularly without losing the value of his knowledge and expertise? If his weird behavior is triggered by stress, telling him about it might just stress him out even more!

Analysis

As you become more and more familiar with the Behavioral Change Map in Chapter 4, you will come to the conclusion that this must be a skill issue. In other words, it is hard to believe that if Terry knew how he looked, and what effect it was having on his potential success, he certainly would not be lacking in motivation to change. So now he needs to learn how.

But how do we tell him? Every professional should always be in some form of a targeted personal or professional development plan. And since Terry is now in a position of meeting with clients, it stands to reason that he might benefit from some interpersonal effectiveness training. We don't need to introduce this with the premise that he looks and acts weird in public. That would only be destructive and put him on the defensive.

Here are a couple of options. You could enroll him in a training program that includes role-playing and videotaping. I don't care how effective you think you are, when you see yourself on video for the first time, it ain't pretty. If this was done by an outside seminar or consulting company, no one would be privy to it but Terry and his trainer.

Another solution is to hire a personal performance coach. This is becoming more and more common for executives who really don't get enough candid and focused feedback. Whether it's for presentation skills, self-awareness, or some other form of development, having a personal coach is like talking to your shrink or your priest. Candor, compassion, and confidentiality can accomplish miracles.

In the meantime, counsel Terry's co-workers on being less cruel and heartless. Maybe they could use a little video taping as well!

Public Affairs

OK, we've been through both forms of sexual harassment now ("Somebody's Got To Do It!" and "Quid Pro Quo *Pro*"), but what about the inter-office affair that is neither a hostile environment nor quid pro quo? It's just an affair!

Hank and Hanna hooked up at an annual offsite staff meeting in Florida, along with a bunch of other staffers, to learn about a new project, hear a "state of the company" address, and to wine and dine on the company expense report. Nothing wrong with a little R&R, huh?

One evening, after everyone had gorged their gullets with booze and brie in a beachside restaurant, it was just too nice a night to resist taking a stroll (stagger) on the beach. For the most part, it was just that, a lot of laughing, a little kidding, and some kicking in the sand. However, as the crowd started to disperse, and people headed back to their rooms, or out to another bar, Hank and Hanna had developed a sort of magnetism. That magnet seemed to be attached to their bellies, because it wasn't long before the sand crabs were seeing some action.

So, what's the problem? Hank and Hanna do not report to each other. They don't even work in the same department! Well, it may have passed unnoticed, had they not decided to continue the action back at work. It never ended.

They would meet before work, God knows where, and walk in looking like the cat that just ate the bird, thinking they were being discreet. They would disappear together at lunch. They would find opportunities to "team build" wherever and whenever possible, but never on company time, nor on company property. So, what's the problem here?

Well, aside from the fact that they are both married, but not to each other, they are also employed by Christian Ministries Foundation, an organization that has clear standards for behavior, clear definitions of right and wrong, and a mission to bring sinners to their knees around the world.

Now what? Is it an employer's right, or even obligation, to interfere with workers' personal lives if it is not infringing on company time or property? Can adultery be against company policy, or is that dictating behavior beyond the job requirements?

Analysis

As is the case in every one of the situations in this book, it is critical that you have the facts before proceeding full speed into the morass that awaits you. So, first be sure that Hank and Hanna are still married (to other people) and then be sure that they are not just really good friends who spend a lot of time together. I know. Some things are obvious. But it is critical to get all the facts first in situations as sensitive and volatile as these.

Let's first address the issue of office romances in general. Contrary to what one might assume, office romances are a lot more successful, and less dangerous, than you might think. And, they're also more serious. Recent research has revealed that more than half of all office romances end in long-term commitments or marriage (ref: Dennis Powers, professor at Southern Oregon University's School of Business). With about eight million Americans expected to get their meat where they get their bread each year, those are much better odds than the success rates of traditional dating relationships.

Now, let's be practical. Discretion is the key. Not that committing adultery discreetly is acceptable, but if you, as employer, decide to intervene into the personal matters of employees, including those that cross over into areas involving morals and values, then you may be opening a Pandora's box of potential problems for yourself and your organization.

Go back to the Behavioral Change Map, and ask yourself if their behavior is costing you anything. I know that sounds rather calloused and maybe even irresponsible, and may not be the point to you personally, but this is a business, not a family. It's not like you can have someone arrested for cheating. You may not like it, but that's reality.

However, once you have confirmed the facts of the relationship, there is nothing wrong with each person's supervisor, and/or the Human Resources officer (in fact, it is probably best to have both present) sitting down with the parties, separately, and reading them the riot act as to their lack of good judgment and discretion. This is fair and appropriate territory for you to pursue. Not the legitimacy of the relationship, but its impact on the organization vis a vis the hubbub and distraction created by their behavior.

Forget policies that prohibit co-workers from dating. They don't work. The only exception to that is when there is a direct reporting relationship or potential for fiduciary collusion, such as a bank manager dating a teller. But in most cases, it isn't worth trying to regulate relationships.

Besides, the corporate benefits of employees romancing one another may be greater than you think. Just ask Southwest Airlines! It has over 1,000 married couples dipping their pens in the company ink. Southwest not only permits such marriages, but even gives an annual "Love Award" recognizing the contribution that one special couple makes to the company. Another example of workplace weddings that work is at the offices of National Public Radio (NPR). Over the years, they have produced over 60 marriages between staffers.

Granted, the Hank and Hanna genre of fishing off the company pier is inappropriate at best, but it can be dealt with discreetly from the employer's end. The best advice is to lay it on the line regarding their lack of judgment and public persona, but then leave it alone unless it becomes a drain on the organization, or if it creates a conflict of interest.

Like it or not, your personal position and concern about the adultery issue is going to have to be put aside. In most cases, the spouse already knows, so it accomplishes nothing from a business or a legal perspective to threaten to spill the beans on the home front, or to prohibit their sticky wicket. It wouldn't accomplish anything but to create even more trauma and further fertilize an already ripe grapevine.[2]

Wanna Buy Some Cookies?

The sign on the main office door said "No Solicitation." It also said vendors and visitors must register with the receptionist. But does that apply to employees, too? Priscilla came in one morning with cases of her daughter's Girl Scout cookies, set them up in the coffee break room along with a sign soliciting co-workers to buy them, and a box to put their money in. No big deal?

Well, it wasn't long before she was walking the halls with order forms for Christmas cards, candy, candles and other holiday paraphernalia for sale for her kids' high school band trip fundraiser. It didn't end there! She was also an Amway and an Avon distributor! She didn't hard sell anyone, but the catalogues were clearly displayed in the reception lobby, the break room and several other high traffic areas with her name and phone number stamped on them. People ordered products; she delivered them to their workplace. How convenient!

---

2. There is an emerging trend on the horizon called "consensual-relationship agreements" in which employers protect themselves from potential sexual harassment litigation by documenting that the relationship is consensual and welcome. The difference between sexual harassment and office romance is that the romance is consensual and welcome, while harassment is not. These "love contracts" can also stipulate that if either party is feeling harassed, that they are obligated to inform management, and can also include an agreement to refrain from inappropriate behavior at work. Time will tell if these agreements work.

Eventually, more and more people tried to avoid Priscilla like the plague. If they saw her coming toward them in the hall, they would ditch into the restroom, or make a sudden U-turn and hide wherever it was safe at the moment. There were a few "loyal" customers who bought a little of something most of the time, either because they were "guilted" into it, or they were high on the conflict-avoidance scale. Whatever the reason, they were easy prey for Priscilla the Pusher.

If you weren't a buyer of her goods, you were still fair game to be recruited into her multi-level marketing network. She was even known to follow people into the restroom to ask if they were interested in making money in their spare time. Priscilla's "spare" time just happened to be at work, i.e., at her real job.

Although no one specifically complained formally about Priscilla's ventures, it had become common knowledge and a common irritant to many. She didn't hide her activities, nor did she think there was anything wrong with "helping others" and "sharing opportunities." What do you think?

Analysis

You have two choices: (isn't that nice, for a change?)

1. Do nothing and just expect people to continue fending for themselves against Priscilla.

2. Counsel Priscilla about her "on-the-job" non-job-related activities and instruct her to cease and desist immediately.

This all boils down to a simple company policy decision. In option #1, you are admitting, by default, that solicitation is an acceptable practice on company time and property, and that it is an individual's choice whether to be receptive to it or not. One downside to this "non-strategy" is that more and more Priscillas and products may develop over time, competition may develop, and eventually a line in the sand will have to be drawn anyway. Not to mention that you may also be making it easier for a union-organizing campaign to take place since your past practice was to allow any type of solicitation. That's another whole book!

If option #2 is chosen, it will be necessary to make sure that Priscilla is not the only offender. This *is* an all-or-nothing proposition. And the best way to intervene fairly and effectively is to adopt a clear, strict and well-communicated policy regarding onsite solicitation. Either no one does it, or the door is open for anyone to do it.

You don't want to put yourself in a position of having to approve or disapprove every case individually. Degrees of abuse should not be the determining factor for intervention. In other words, you cannot say that one person can sell Christmas cookies once per year but someone else cannot sell everything from soup to nuts the rest of the year. This is a line that you just can't draw because it is an ever-moving and highly subjective target. Between all-or-nothing, nothing is clearly the easier and cleaner alternative.

Carpal Tunnel Crapola

Christine was a data entry clerk who spent significant periods of time at the keyboard entering customer information into the company computer. She was both fast and accurate in her keyboarding skills.

As time went on, she complained that the extended hours at the keyboard were causing her fingers and hands to cramp up. The company sought the counsel of a workplace ergonomic consultant, who recommended wrist rests, optimum workspace angles, and other preventative measures which the company adopted for everyone, not just Christine.

Christine, however, was accommodated even further. She was allowed to take extended breaks away from data entry to do other tasks that did not require similar, repetitive hand motion whenever she felt the pain coming on. She was on the honor system in this regard, and it didn't take long for her to be off the job more than on. Eventually, there just wasn't enough side work to accommodate her apparently impending disability.

Out of the blue, Christine appeared in the Human Resources department one morning with a letter from her doctor stating that she would have to take medical leave for an indefinite period of time to both rest and to rehabilitate her developing carpal tunnel syndrome. She then went to the local workers' compensation bureau and filed a claim for her workplace injury.

The company honored the doctor's recommendation; they put her on fully paid short term disability leave, with the requirement that her doctor report her progress on a bi-weekly basis. Days turned into weeks, weeks turned into months. And to make matters worse, it came to the company's attention that Christine was not only a master keyboardist, but she was also a prolific and profitable seamstress, needlepoint and crochet artist. What was even more ironic was the way in which the company found out about her transferable dexterity skills.

As part of a new product promotion, the marketing department contracted with a local logo-wear company to design and produce golf shirts with the new product logo embroidered on them. Guess whom the logo-wear company sub-contracted with to do their logo stitching? Yep! Crafty Christine!

Essentially, they were paying Christine twice…once for *not* working her regular job and once *for* working an even more tedious job on the side! Work which, if she truly was developing carpal tunnel syndrome, would further aggravate the alleged injury that was exacerbated by her data entry work on the keyboard in the first place! This is truly a case of adding insult to injury! Now what?

Analysis

Chris "the Carp" and her doc told you one set of "facts." But you learned that those "facts" are untrue. To be kind, "the Carp" is operating contrary to her medical profile to obtain benefits (money) under false pretenses! That's lying and grounds for immediate discharge for dishonesty.

But be sure to verify her lying, so you can prove it if and when she claims a retaliatory firing. If she does, your answer is, "We fired her because she lied to us about the existence and severity of her medical condition to get time off and money from us under false pretenses."

Pretty straightforward, huh? If, however you lack the backbone or desire to fire her (maybe she is just so valuable?), and you don't mind having a liar and a fraud in your midst, you can require an immediate independent medical exam to confirm that if she can crochet, she can keyboard. It might even be easier if you call her and tell her what you already know, and hope that she comes clean on her own. Up to you!

Is it Work, or is it Play.com?

Jack had to go out of town. In the meantime, his was the only computer that had the report that his boss, Pete, needed to access while he was gone, so he emailed Jack, got his password, and asked him to walk him through his computer to find it. In the process of logging on and digging into Jack's computer, Pete encountered a few distractions and diversions along the way. From pop-up ads to numerous non-business icons, questionable bookmarks, and a whole host of suspicious junk on Jack's computer, his was a party machine!

After Pete got the report he needed, he couldn't help but to do a little more digging. The more he dug, the more non-business activity he discovered. Jack was not only paying his personal bills online, but he was also having a good old time visiting online casinos, dating sites, and whatever else you could imagine to "pass the time" at work.

At first, Pete felt a little guilty, having dug around into Jack's computer, but the more he thought about it, the more angry he got. But how could he confront Jack without telling him that he was prying into his computer, well beyond just looking up the report he needed? Did Pete cross the line here? Does he have the right to look at Jack's "personal" business?

Analysis

OK, so what's wrong with a little game of solitaire while sitting through a boring conference call, or while a vendor drones on and on about their innovative business solutions? Maybe nothing. But, that's your call. In other words, as an employer, you must determine when you feel the cost/benefit justifies it or should prohibit it. It can range anywhere from zero tolerance, to "have at it!"

But let's talk specifically about Jack. He's not just playing an occasional game of hearts. He's engaged in personal business, and we're not just talking about online bill paying, either. Even if his activities do not cross the line into bad taste, which they probably do, it is obvious that he is spending way too much time *not doing his real job!* Hello?

Many people misinterpret the whole spectrum of rights that we enjoy in society as being absolutely transferable to the workplace. They are not! Rights like privacy, protection from search and seizure, etc., are intended to protect us from our own government, not our employer. An employer's decision to dig through an employee's emails in computer storage does not violate any provisions of the Electronic Communications Privacy Act either. This law bans the "interception" only if it occurs at the time of transmission and exempts the owner, (i.e., the employer), of an email system from any claim alleging an illegal "seizure" of stored emails. Like it or not, you do not own that computer. You do not own your locker. You do not own your desk. If you want to play blackjack online, buy your own computer and do it from home!

Pete has nothing to apologize for. He is perfectly within his rights as an agent of his employer to call Jack to the carpet, boot up his computer and ask, "What's up with this?" However, it would probably be prudent to assume that Jack may just be the tip of the Internet iceberg.

If you have no formal policy or procedure in place that addresses Internet and email protocols, now's probably the time to develop one.

Activities such as Jack's fall into a category called "system slop," which is defined by how far people can push the limits of formal structure, policies, procedures, etc., without getting into trouble. How much system slop exists in your organization? In other words, how far can people go beyond the realm of reasonableness and still not be in violation of some rule? Human beings have a unique ability to figure out pretty quickly where the limits are, and then play right to the edge.

Every organization has some degree of system slop, and some of it can actually be positive. It is virtually impossible to regulate every conceivable behavior, and it isn't advisable even to try. No one wants to work in a police state. Everyone needs a little release now and then. It could be as simple as a two-minute game of trashcan basketball, or sharing an email cartoon. One cannot, nor should not, try to regulate behavior to that degree. It's not only harmless but can actually be necessary to keep a semblance of sanity. It can be both liberating and invigorating.

So, once you clean up Jack's act, there are several possible approaches that will curb future such abuses. First, develop and disseminate a very clear statement of policy as to what is acceptable and what is not. It can be very clear. But again, it is your decision.

What kind of operation or culture do you want? Anything goes? No holds barred? Or, work is work and play is play, and never the twain shall meet?

Assuming you want something closer to the latter, you not only need to specify exactly what is acceptable, but also how you are going to ensure that no one crosses the line without putting everyone into bondage. In other words, it is one thing to read the riot act, but quite another to enforce it. Once the new rules are laid out, it is essential that people know you mean it, but with minimal cost and disruption.

For example, if you had a zero-tolerance drug policy, but never tested anyone, you would have nothing more than a toothless tiger. However, you don't have to go to the opposite extreme and create a Gestapo state either, testing everyone all the time. That's why random testing is so effective. It's like a lottery. You never know when your number might come up!

The same principle applies here. In behavioral terms, it is called the "Sentinel Effect." Have you ever seen video cameras up in the corners of retail stores? Whether they have film in them or not, the mere presence is a deterrent to theft, like a sentinel. If you were a burglar wandering around a nice neighborhood planning your next heist, would you pick the house that has a big security sign in the front yard? It's a game of poker that's not worth playing and a hand that's not worth calling.

Again, you make the call. But with all the viruses, parasites, and other stuff that can really junk up your servers, not to mention the loss of productivity and laissez-faire culture you are fostering, it just makes good business sense to be very clear on this one.

The X-pense Account

Richard was a field marketing executive who called on the company's various regional offices to consult with their marketing representatives to help them develop their local strategies and to ensure consistency with the overall corporate marketing objectives. He was a well-dressed, articulate, and personable young man. He was also single and marketing himself as well.

The bad news was that he was on the road a lot. The good news was that he had a lot of latitude about when and where he went, as long as objectives were met within budget and on time. As in any company, he had an expense account. And, as in most companies, there were policies and guidelines about allowable expenses and limits.

One day, the accounting department conducted a random audit of one of Dick's expense accounts. This was standard procedure and just good accounting practice to quality-check expense reimbursements, receipts, etc. He was not being targeted for any reason.

Upon reviewing a hotel receipt, there appeared to be several "miscellaneous" charges, some of which were substantial in amount. In fact, upon cross-referencing with past receipts from the same bed and breakfast, the room charge seemed to vary widely. One time it was $75.00 per night, and another it was as much as $175.00 per night. Same room, same B&B. Additionally, Dick's phone charges seemed to be excessive at times.

When the accounting clerk called the B&B to ask about their rate structure, miscellaneous charges, etc., she was referred to the owner, who acted rather sheepish and, at times, downright evasive. Upon further questioning and subsequent pressure, the owner finally "fessed up" and said that because Richard was a frequent guest, she agreed to do him some favors in exchange for his customer loyalty. Marketing to the marketer? Favors? What kind of favors?

Bottom line: Dick was ordering more than room service and charging it to the room. Many B&B's lump the meals and the room charge together into one price. This is not unusual. But this one bundled massages, dial-a-date, porno videos and just about anything else that would "satisfy" the customer—in this case, Dick.

The proprietor admitted embarrassment and said that they only did it for Dick because he was rather adamant about his needs and the expectation that they should help get them satisfied via his expense account, and she didn't want to lose his business. He is one of their best customers, after all!

On paper he was only charging room and board and phone. And as we all know, padding an expense account is no new thing. In fact, phone charges are reimbursable, as are bundled room and board charges. Even drinking one's dinner is a common practice for some business travelers.

Whether Dick spent his meal allowance on beef or bourbon, who would know? It's a restaurant charge! And who knows if an employee really tipped the valet five bucks? Where do you draw the line? He didn't technically exceed any spending limits, didn't break any laws, and what he does on his own time is his own business, isn't it?

Analysis

Nope. Dick, who has been making himself Rich at your expense, to remain employed, has a duty to follow common sense standards of behavior, including ethical behavior. Under the applicable business reimbursement policy and guidelines—applied in a common sense fashion—Dick had the right to reimbursement for *reasonable* out-of-pocket expenses for his overnight trips. That meant reasonable lodging, food, and car expenses, plus *legitimate* miscellaneous expenses.

It's your call as to whether you give him a second chance or not. If his performance is otherwise exemplary you can always have a "Come to Jesus" meeting with him (not literally!), put him on probation, and keep him on a short leash for a while.

Or you can just dump Dick altogether. "Miscellaneous," by no stretch of logic or ethics means "X-rated" personal enjoyment expenses. By getting reimbursed for and attempting to get reimbursed for "X-rated" expenses, our boy Dick acted contrary to common sense standards of ethical behavior and may deserve to hit the road, this time without expense reimbursements—or a job!

This is a judgment call. But whatever you decide, just be sure you are consistent in how you apply the policy to others. If Dick is a water-walker and makes you tons of money in sales, then you may want to issue a warning before throwing him to the wolves. But that does not mean that he is exempt from being a professional and behaving as such, which includes following both the letter and the spirit of company policies, procedures and protocols.

The Two-Year Head Cold

Alex was a hard charger. A real go-getter. When he sunk his teeth into a project, it got done. His energy level was unmatched by anyone. He was a bit moody at times, but that's a small price to pay for the incredible results he consistently attained. And now his hard work was about to be rewarded.

The CEO had seen him in several meetings and on special projects in the past, and was impressed with his ambition and style. He was looking for someone to head up a major new account, and he had one guy in mind...Alex!

"Alex has the kind of drive and energy that will WOW this client!" he said. He talked with Alex's current department head, Mary, and with Connie, the Human Resources manager, about the promotion. Although neither of them put the brakes on the CEO's enthusiasm, there was guarded optimism about such a proposal. The HR manager asked for some time to check Alex's personnel history and to get his ducks in a row before "blessing" the final decision. He was obviously trying to buy some time.

When the CEO left the room, Mary and Connie conferred. Both knew what the other was thinking without saying a word. Alex's hard charging, go-getter behavior was not just rooted in a passion for his position, but in a cocaine addiction. The CEO's exposure to Alex was limited to the occasional staff meeting or project briefing. He wasn't aware of the fact that Alex has had an unexplainable head cold for the past two years. Not to mention the fact that he has to go to the bathroom more often than a seagull on Ex-Lax.®

Granted, no one has officially confirmed Alex's addiction. His performance has been exemplary. He hasn't missed work, and with the exception of his outward symptomatic behavior, no one would have a clue, as the CEO has clearly demonstrated. Should they approve the move, or spill the beans? Are there any other options?

Analysis #1

There are several issues and considerations in these kinds of cases, and even some different legal philosophies on how to approach a drug or alcohol abuse situation. Here's the first one, according to Mr. Eugene K. Connors, Esq. of the law firm Reed Smith, LLP.

Mary and Connie should spill the (coca) beans here, but not too quickly. Suspecting Alex of cocaine abuse is not *knowing* or being able to *prove* it as true. So Mary and Connie need to use the extra time they bought to investigate and *prove* cocaine abuse by Alex. If their company has a written drug policy, what happens next should be easy. Running frequently to a bathroom is suspicious behavior, typically enough to satisfy any reasonable cause or suspicion required under most drug policies to drug-test an existing employee. If Alex refuses to be tested, he is subject to discharge or other discipline for insubordination (for refusing to cooperate in a reasonable investigation), and, in addition or alternatively, depending upon the language of the drug policy, the refusal may count as an automatic "positive" drug test result.

But let's assume he takes the test. He will pass it or flunk it. If he passes it, there is no proof of cocaine abuse at this point, and Mary and Connie can and should proceed with the proposed promotion. If Alex flunks, they should subject him to rehabilitation, reinstatement on a last chance basis, and future random testing, or discharge him, again depending upon the wording of the policy itself.

But what if there is no written drug policy? Even so, Mary and Connie's company probably has a rule against drug use at work. Therefore, they still should have the right to drug-test him. How and why? To investigate whether there has been a violation of the rule, again stemming from his suspicious runs to the bathroom.

But what if there is no written rule? Not a problem. Let's not forget our common-sense standards of ethical behavior. By any stretch of logic, any employee knows or should know that he or she has no right to show up for work or otherwise be in work related activities while under the influence of forbidden drugs. Instead an employee's duty is to perform at 100% when scheduled to work. That means, once again, Mary and Connie can test Alex and take appropriate action consistent with the drug test results.

Analysis #2

Another school of thought takes quite a different stance, based more exclusively on job performance. In other words, if Alex is performing his job well, some legal advisors recommend a more hands-off approach. A good place to start is to understand the concept of "reasonable suspicion" and its ramifications on testing.

According to Jonathan A. Segal, Esq. a partner in Wolf, Block, Schorr, and Solis-Cohen's Employment Services Practice Group, reasonable suspicion tests can be divided into two categories. The first are those situations in which an employee's job performance is affected by the use of drugs or abuse of alcohol, even though the employee is not under the influence while at work. The second set of circumstances are those in which the employee is actually under the influence of drugs or alcohol while on duty. According to Mr. Segal, drug testing is never justified in the first set of cases and only rarely in the second.

Testing employees who manifest behaviors indicative of drug or alcohol abuse is unnecessary, insufficient, and unwise, according to Mr. Segal, even when the employer has reason to believe that performance problems are related to substance abuse. Testing in these circumstances is unnecessary because the reason for the performance deficiency is of no concern to the employer. The employer should be responding to the performance problem through its progressive discipline and/or corrective counseling procedures without inquiring as to its underlying cause. While drugs and alcohol clearly have an adverse effect on the workplace, one of the dangers of screening is its focus on the cause instead of the effect.

A question that arises frequently is whether supervisors should mention their belief that the performance problem may be related to the abuse of alcohol or drugs. Of course, this confrontation may serve as a valuable catalyst for the employee to seek rehabilitation. But it may also backfire against the employer, because if the employee denies having a drug or alcohol problem, which is likely since denial is part of the disease, and if adverse action is subsequently taken against the employee, the employee will assume, and claim, that the employer's action was based on the misguided perception that the employee was a substance abuser.

A less pristine but safer alternative to confronting the employee specifically about a believed drug or alcohol problem is to let the employee know that his or her job is on the line and encourage the person to seek help if there is any underlying problem that may be causing the performance deficiency, without specifically mentioning substance abuse.

According to Mr. Segal, testing employees when there is unacceptable workplace conduct or performance is not only unnecessary but also insufficient. While drug and alcohol abuse can cause performance deficiencies, there are a number of patterns not related to substance abuse that could be the cause, including family problems, marital problems, physical health problems, mental health problems, workplace stress, and even financial problems.

In this regard, drug testing is a dangerously myopic approach because there is an implication that when an employee tests negative, the conduct that gave rise to the test is no longer a problem. After all, if the cause for the test were a problem in and of itself, there would have been no need for the test, which is in fact usually the case. It should not matter to an employer whether an employee's unacceptable on-the-job performance is because of a drug, marital problems, or financial problems. Regardless of the cause, the employer's focus should be on the effect.

Finally, drug and alcohol testing may be counterproductive. That is, it may preclude the employer from discharging an employee whom it otherwise could have discharged. Individuals who are dependent on drugs or alcohol are considered disabled under virtually every state law. Consequently, an adverse employment decision cannot be made against them unless their condition is job-related. Of course, if the use of drugs or alcohol have a negative impact on their job performance, then the dependency is job-related.

There is, however, one legal wrinkle. Under state handicap discrimination laws, a condition is not job-related if, with a reasonable accommodation, the job-relatedness of the condition can be eliminated. In the context of drug and alcohol dependency, some courts have held that the reasonable accommodation requirement imposes on employers an obligation to provide employees with an opportunity for rehabilitation prior to discharge. The courts are much less likely to impose this obligation on the employer if the employer does not learn that the employee had a drug or alcohol problem until after his discharge.

Let's get back to our specific case of Alex. As far as we know, there are no job-performance issues on which we can hang our hat. However, there are suspicions, based upon his "hyper-alertness," his constant head cold, and his frequent trips to the can, that there may be something going on.

According to Mr. Segal, in those situations in which the employer has reason to believe the employee is under the influence, but the conclusion is not inescapable and there is inadequate evidence of impact on job performance to justify discipline, these are the ONLY kinds of situations in which drug and alcohol testing is appropriate. Limiting testing to these circumstances will mean that for most employers, its policy of testing employees when there is reasonable suspicion will involve hardly any testing at all.

But just because reasonable-suspicion testing will be the exception and not the rule, it does not follow that an employer can afford to have a substance abuse policy that does not authorize reasonable-suspicion testing. To the contrary, notwithstanding its limited application, reasonable-suspicion testing is a critical component of a comprehensive substance abuse control program.

The Customer is Not Always Right?

Lucretia is our customer. Well, at least her company is. And a relatively good customer at that, in terms of their purchase volume and the length of time they have been doing business with us. But it comes at a price. And Lucretia is the price. She is a first class _ _ _ _ _ (you can fill in the blanks yourself…just make sure it is bad!)

No matter how long she does business with us, and no matter how well she knows us, she seems to get some weird pleasure out of making us jump through unnecessary, sadistic hoops. Sometimes the same hoops, over and over. And she is always trying to get something for nothing. Unless she can find a way to make us squirm and give in on something, she isn't happy. In fact, she isn't even happy then. She's just a miserable human being.

Because Lucretia's company (OK, her Daddy's company) has been a customer since the early days of the company's founding, when we would have put up with anything for cash flow, we feel like we are obligated to put up with her shenanigans. But not all of our employees see it that way. In fact, fewer and fewer are feeling charitable toward Lucretia. It seems that Lucretia is even more abusive when she encounters a new employee who has yet to be "baptized" by her. It's as if she has to put them in their place right from the start, to let them know who's the boss.

She asks for special reports; wants unusual payment plans, terms, and conditions; submits last-minute orders and changes and wants them fulfilled by the original deadline; and the list goes on. It's a known fact that she puts unreasonable demands and deadlines on staff for things that she just lets sit for weeks anyway, and then doesn't even need or use them.

It has been suggested that we go to her superiors and blow the whistle on her, but she reports to the owner, and the owner is, yes...her Daddy. To make matters even worse, she is the heir apparent to the family fortune, so going to her boss (Daddy) could be the kiss of death, if not now, at least later. You deal with Lucretia, or you don't deal!

Since the company's account base is growing and manpower resources are stretched thin to accommodate newer and more appreciative and profitable customers, people are becoming more and more vocal about the stress and brain drain caused by Lucretia. Are she and her company really worth the agony? Is the customer always right?

Analysis

On a purely cost-benefit basis, this customer costs a lot more per sales dollar than any other customer. She is high-maintenance. Even though the rule of thumb is that it costs five times more to get a new customer than to keep an existing one, Lucretia may be the exception to that rule. It might actually be a better use of our time to woo new customers than to continue to schmooze her. But it just doesn't seem logical for a company to turn business away—especially a long term customer. Does it?

Well, before you throw the baby out with the bath water, start with a "Can we talk?" meeting with Lucretia. Cater to her need for dominance and superiority by taking an apologetic tone, saying: "We are sorry that we have not been able to meet your expectations, and have come to the conclusion that there is nothing that we seem to be able to do to satisfy you." Then put it in her lap for a response.

She will either see the light of day, and may even respect you more for the revelation, or she will continue to be difficult and offer no suggestions other than to continue to cater to her unreasonableness.

Assuming the worst, i.e., the latter scenario, and you have decided that this is not negotiable and that something truly must change in your business relationship with Lucretia in order to continue doing business with her, you must then be willing and able to take the risk of talking to Daddy. In other words, he who can walk, has the power. Rather than just saying, "We don't want to do business with you anymore," as a last resort, ask for a meeting with "the owner" and lay it on the line. Once again, use the counseling sandwich approach:

1. Open the meeting acknowledging your long, mutually rewarding history together, how much you have valued it, and how you have tried to satisfy them at all costs because of that. Then move to:

2. The issue. However, depersonalize it. Rather than crucify Lucretia, which would be fun and cathartic, admit that you do not believe you have been able to satisfy them recently, and that you are at a loss as to how to do so, and that you need their help to identify how you can "get things right the first time" and not waste their time. This should open the door for specifics, which they will ask for, rather than you spilling your guts on the table up front.

3. Once the issues are identified (such as change orders, repeat requests, etc.) either Daddy and/or Lucretia will have to own up, or you can tell them that you regret not being able to be their supplier anymore, but that you will be glad to find an alternate vendor for them so they are not left in the lurch.

4. Now here's the fun part. Assuming the answer to #3 is yes, that the best alternative would be to find an alternative vendor, this is when you direct them to your competition. In every crisis there is an opportunity! Let Lucretia drain their resources for a while.

Just a final footnote: Before doing any of this, make sure your employees (the ones who despise this customer the most, and who have the most to gain by your turning them loose) understand exactly why you are making this unusual business decision to let a customer go, and that this does not open the door for them to throw every difficult customer under a bus.

Also tell them that if you are willing to bite the bullet and turn this customer away, then it is incumbent upon them to help you find new customers to fill the void. Nothing is free in this life, and you're doing them a real favor here. Now they owe you one!

Pets are People Too

Annie loves her dogs. Annie loves her cats. Annie loves animals. Annie is married without children. Or is she? Not if you ask her! Annie's employer is actually one of the more liberal and progressive companies in town, but still not liberal enough for Annie's liking. They provide onsite daycare for employees' dependent children, they have a flexible benefits plan, and even onsite personal services such as dry cleaning pickup and delivery, massages, and other new age perks and privileges for their workers.

So what's the problem? Well, Annie's pets are as important to her as other employees' children are to them. When they are ill, she wants family medical leave. She would even like to have dependent medical coverage for them if she could. When her husband works day shift, she wants day care for Fido and Fifi. She even talks to them on the phone at least once a day (her husband calls, says they miss her, and holds the phone to their ears while Annie talks doggie/kitty talk to them). One time, her assistant even interrupted an onsite client conference to beckon Annie out of the meeting to answer such a call, which the client could overhear.

So, where do you draw the line in the kitty litter?

Analysis

Animals are not people. Easy enough? There is a reason why employers do not provide the same benefits to employees' pets as they do to children and partners. Cost and common sense! Not that an employer couldn't self-fund such a thing, but it doesn't make a whole lot of business sense, which is why Annie will be hard pressed to find alternative employment with such benefits. But if she can, let her! That's the beauty of living in a free society! Employment-at-will can be a wonderful thing!

Regarding her obsession manifesting itself in front of clients and disrupting the normal workflow, this is a performance counseling issue (see Behavioral Change Map). It has nothing to do with equal opportunity for animals or compassion for our furry little friends. It is no different than expecting other employees to make proper arrangements for other personal matters in such a way as to minimize disruption or distractions at work. It's called planning and self-management. Shape up or ship out, Annie (maybe on an Ark?)!

Helen the Hypochondriac

Helen comes in handy at times, especially if you're in need of a home remedy or alternative medical advice. At other times, she is truly a headache. You see, Helen has a cure for anything. Too bad none of them work for her, because she is always suffering from some new malady. One day it might be sick building syndrome; the next day it is seasonal affect disorder (SAD); she even brought in a feng shui consultant to correct the karma in her cubicle (see Feng Shui Phoebe).

Ordinarily, one could just ignore such obsessions. But with Helen, she thrusts them upon everyone else. If you sneeze, she comes running into your office with zinc tablets. If you look unusually tired, she is counseling you about some new herb you should be taking. She's even been known to apply accupressure to people without even being asked or given permission.

She's not selling anything; she's just preaching it. But there is an air of judgmentalism when one does not heed her sage advice. If all this stuff is so good for you, why is Helen always ill? Is her behavior an excessive intrusion on others? Is some intervention necessary here?

Analysis

Essentially Helen has a good heart—maybe not literally, but figuratively! Her intentions are good. She's just a pain in the rear (for which she may also have a cure!). Seriously, with the exception of her putting her hands on someone without permission, her behavior is not intolerable.

Granted, she is either unaware or unconcerned about how she is perceived, but that is true of a lot of people—maybe even you! Remember low self-monitoring in Chapter 1? So, unless she is dispensing drugs or crossing the line of one's personal space (i.e., touching), get over it! You don't have to take her advice or her remedies. And who knows, maybe she has a few good ones up her sleeve!

As is true in almost every case, the bigger issue boils down to job performance. If her behavior is taking her away from her duties, or keeping others from theirs, then intervention is justified, not because of her quasi-medical practice, but because she and her patients should be working! Focus on that issue, if necessary, and the other issues should take care of themselves.

Human Billboards

God Bless America! Save the Whales! Abortion Kills! Vote No on Issue X! There are enough causes, campaigns and crises in this world that anyone can identify with something. But is it appropriate to have them emblazoned on your bosom at work? According to Neon Leon, it certainly is.

Acme Bio-Micro-Solutions is like most other companies that care about social causes and want to be good corporate citizens. They have blood drives, the annual United Way campaign, walks for the cure, and other corporately correct endeavors. They provide buttons and banners to promote them and even give people time off the job to support them.

But, who decides which cause is worth championing? What about the union activist who distributes lapel buttons to contract holdouts to "Just Say No" to the latest company offer? What about the right-to-life group within the company who wears "abortion is murder" buttons? What about political campaign buttons from all extremes of the political spectrum? What about the gay population that is lobbying for domestic partner benefits at work?

Are these disruptive activities that should be stopped, or just examples of the right to free speech, freedom of expression, freedom of religion, etc.? Can a company dictate what an employee can wear on his/her clothing? And, who decides what stays, and what goes?

Analysis

Remember Al Naturale? Remember Walking Art? Employees of a private (non-government) employer have no freedoms or rights of expression or speech. Plus, every employer has a legal duty to keep a workplace safe. That duty stems from federal or state safety laws like OSHA (Occupational Safety and Health Act) or court-created tort (Don't be negligent!) law.

To allow Leon, or any employee, to "advertise" positions certain to cause dissention, if not outright fights, would be dumb for any employer. That is why companies, by written or unwritten common-sense standards of behavior, can and should require employees to "keep quiet" or "calm down" controversial, political, religious, and other potentially dissention-causing "sales pitches." That employer approach prevents most problems, from abortion disputes to XXX T-shirts and other potentially volatile slogans and messages.

But what of union messages, like "Ma Bell is a cheap mother?" Under our labor laws, an employer cannot say "no" to such pro-union or even anti-union messages during an employee's free working hours, like meals and breaks, unless the messages are in seriously bad taste. And "Ma Bell" is at least pushing that line. But an employer can stop such messages during scheduled working time, so long as the employer forbids T-shirt and similar messages like "Be Happy" and "Just Do It."

Employers cannot have it both ways. If they forbid all messages, they can forbid "union" messages when employees are supposed to be working. But if they allow some messages, they have to allow at least non-controversial messages that have a "union tone" to them.

Long Live the Confederacy!

Buford was a good ole boy. He was a member of an organization of direct descendents of Confederate veterans and displayed it proudly on his toolbox with a flag on every side. He felt pretty safe about it since the toolbox was his personal property, and also served as his personal affirmation of his Constitutional right to freedom of speech.

Unfortunately, some of Buford's black co-workers saw it differently, particularly in the context of a heated debate in the state of South Carolina as to its racist underpinnings. They went to their employer and asked the company to intervene.

Buford's supervisor asked him to remove the stickers from his toolbox, and even offered to buy him a new one, so he could keep his confederate-laden toolbox at home.

Buford's response? No deal! His pride was not for sale. What's an employer to do now?

Analysis

On the surface, this case may appear to be the same as "Human Bill-boards," but it is not. Bottom line, Buford can be fired for violating the company's anti-harassment policy, if they have one. Buford's claim that he is merely exercising his Constitutional right to free speech, protected by the First Amendment, does not fly.

Buford's employer is not seeking to interfere with his right to fly the Confederate flag, or with participating in the cause in his personal life. They are, however, refusing to tolerate the display of his political beliefs in the workplace, especially when it creates legitimate claims of racial harassment. Remove the flags, or remove Buford. Take your toolbox and go home.

System Tester Sam

Do you know what a qwertyuiop is? If you read my first book, *Get Weird!*, you would. If you didn't, shame on you! Look at the top row of keys on your computer keyboard, or if you are a militant technology holdout, look at your typewriter. What do you see? Yes, a totally illogical arrangement of letters that you are expected to learn and use. Bottom line: An organizational qwertyuiop is anything that makes no sense, is outdated and/or illogical, but continues because "that's the way we've always done it!"

In an organization, a qwertyuiop might be a report that no one reads, or a committee that has outlived its value, or a policy that costs more than it saves, but has become a sacred cow. Get it? Well, Sam gets it, and he has made it a personal crusade to expose his company's warts on a regular basis. To him, sacred cows make great steaks!

Sam is a very high-results-oriented individual and has a strong track record in his department. He actually has developed quite a reputation for being able to get things done, going around the bureaucracy, and leading other successful crusades, which has served him well so far. He is a master at manipulating the informal power structure. But this time, he may have gone too far.

Specifically, he and his peers are supposed to send in a weekly report every Friday to detail their week's activities, progress, etc. Not a big deal, but they also have to compile a monthly report due by the second working day of each month for the prior month, then a quarterly report and ultimately an annual report. See the rub here?

Well, rather than "work the system" and try to get his company to see the waste and illogic at play here (Sam already knows that would be a futile effort anyway) he decided to prove a point, that nobody reads all these reports anyway. So, in one of his quarterly reports he decided to make a mockery of it by saying things like, "If you are reading this report, you must not have read my prior three monthly reports," or, "This is a test; it is only a test; if there was any real news, you would have already known about it by reading my last three monthly reports and my last 12 weekly reports," etc.

The sad thing is, the only person who ever really appreciated his satire was his assistant, because she is the one who typed and distributed it for him. He was right! No one read it! So he made his point, but no one knew. What fun is that?

So, being the maverick that he was, and now feeling doubly and justifiably cocky, he decided to take it one step further. He went to his boss's office and the conversation went something like this:

Sam: "Hey boss, did you get my quarterly report?"

Boss: "Yes."

Sam: "Was it okay?"

Boss: "Yes."

Sam: "Did you actually read it?"

Boss: "Well, I scanned it."

Sam: "Well, I think you might want to read it again. Here's another copy."

Boss: Reads the first few lines, turns beat red, looks up and says, "Why did you do such a thing?

Sam: "To make a point. The same point I have been trying to make for ages, but no one will listen. That these reports are a complete waste of time because no one reads them."

Boss: "But *my* boss gets a copy of these!"

Sam: "Has he said anything about it?"

Boss: "Well, ...no."

Sam: "My point exactly!"

Boss: "You are going to get into big trouble if you continue to do these types of things, Sam!"

Sam: "Big trouble? For trying to save the company time and money? For increasing productivity? For improving morale? Do you realize how many people hate these reports as much as I do? Do you realize that every Friday, and every second day of the month, and every quarter, and every January everyone in this company has to stop doing productive work to generate reports that not only have to be typed, but copied, collated, stapled, routed, filed, and eventually destroyed, and that no one reads? We have been on a cost-cutting kick for as long as I can remember. We have had lay-offs, a hiring freeze, benefits cuts, and have taken all kinds of belt-tightening measures that have destroyed morale. Here is an opportunity to save money and boost morale at the same time. And I am going to get into big trouble? You should be giving me an award for this! I'll take one tenth of the savings and retire!"

What does the boss do now?

Analysis

Well, as you have probably learned by now, the answer is "it depends!" If you are a traditional, insecure boss, you give Sam hell, discipline him, and move him through the progressive discipline process with two possible outcomes: correct his behavior or face eventual termination. What a waste that would be for everyone. That's a lose–lose.

Deep down, Sam is not really a "trouble maker." Sane people do not get out of bed in the morning with the conscious objective of being a jerk. Sam's behavior is rooted in an attempt to actually improve things. Granted, his means are a little rough, but if the boss can park his ego for a few minutes and look at Sam's intentions, he would discover that they are actually positive for the organization.

And perhaps if there had been a mechanism in place for him (and others) to air their frustrations and/or to submit their cost-saving and revenue-generating ideas, such extreme measures would not be necessary. It is called "Creative Dissatisfaction." You will learn about this concept in more detail in Chapter 3, "What's *IN* with High-Performers?"

When a bright, conscientious, and caring employee becomes frustrated with the status quo and has no outlet by which to be heard, the energy becomes negative and eventually must be directed somewhere. Short of quitting the company, it may develop into cynicism, bitterness, and in Sam's case, is ultimately expressed by testing and poking at the system.

If you really want to take the wind out of Sam's sails, thank him for his observation and promise to look into the situation. And if you can respond by eliminating some of the redundant reports, you give him credit and then set up a more formal mechanism for him and others to submit future ideas in a more professional and productive way. It's called gain-sharing, and is a win–win!

Between you and him, you can still express your disappointment in his behavior, but you should also acknowledge his motivation and the value of his contribution and admit that you wish there had been a

better way for such insights to be shared without risking embarrassment for both of you. Sam will be so shocked that you didn't publicly
lynch him that he may start to feel better about you and the company,
and think twice about the way he airs his frustrations in the future. You
are no longer the enemy in his mind!

But it is up to you to make sure that he, and others, do not have to
resort to such measures in the future. Discipline and/or termination in
this case could be a losing proposition for everyone.

Otto versus Oblivious

Otto is a creative, hard working marketing specialist, in spite of the
mutual hatred that exists between him and his boss, Irene. Otto's hatred
is not completely baseless, however. He has to be completely self-
motivated because Irene does everything possible to demean and
demoralize him. She has not only made it clear that she has no respect
for sales and marketing people in general, but Otto makes a great target, and anytime he proposes anything new, she shoots him down. It
has reached a point where they cannot, and will not, even be in the
same room together.

As a result, Irene goes nowhere near his cubicle. In the meantime,
Otto's cubicle has become a den of disdain, with pictures of Irene as
the bull's eye in a target, slanderous slogans about her being a "narcissistic ignoramus" and a plethora of other "I hate the boss!" self-moti-
vating graffiti to 1) serve as catharsis for his anger, and 2) to publicize
and take advantage of the fact that she will never see it anyway because
she avoids Otto like the plague. This is an ironic attempt to get the
respect of his peers by being disrespectful of his boss.

Unfortunately, his peers aren't the only ones who see it. Outside
vendors, customers, and consultants who have to visit with Otto and
the marketing department can't help but see it as well. It's an embarrassment to many of Otto's co-workers, but they feel helpless in going

to Irene about it, for obvious reasons. They would, in effect, be pointing out her spinelessness. Can this be ignored?

Analysis

No. It would be nice to just end there, but some explaining is necessary. Irene is at least as culpable as Otto in this case. In fact, more so! As a manager, she is responsible for both setting the tone and taking action where necessary, and she has done neither.

Additionally, Irene's boss must be held accountable as well. Where is s/he? It looks like there is a culture of denial and avoidance, at least in this department. And since this behavior is visible to outsiders, including customers, there is no excuse for tolerating it, regardless of how valuable and creative Otto may be. You may love his work, but you cannot love this abhorrent behavior.

As a co-worker or co-manager, someone should blow the whistle with either Irene's boss or with Human Resources. If enough people bring it to the attention of an internal third party, a critical mass will develop that cannot be denied, and no one person is being hung out to dry.

Once the issue has been exposed, it is then incumbent upon Irene's boss and/or Human Resources to bring Otto's cubicle décor and decorum to a screeching halt, and to give Irene an ultimatum as to fulfilling her supervisory responsibilities. It's her job, period!

Even though Otto's behavior is tacky and unprofessional, it is ultimately Irene's responsibility to deal with it. She needs to grow some giblets and face the facts. After all, what does she have to lose? Otto hates her anyway!

Feng Shui Phoebe

Phoebe is a "New Age" employee. She is an enlightened web-master who is always into the latest right-brained, spiritual movement. First it was aromatherapy, in which she burned strange oils and incense in her cubicle. Then it was acupressure. You don't want to know what she did with that.

But now she is a disciple of Feng Shui, which is based on a Chinese philosophy of life in which everything from relationships, to health, to career success can be influenced by the position or direction of your furniture, the color of your walls, and numerous other esoteric variables of one's physical environment.

Ironically, Phoebe found out about Feng Shui at a conference to which the company sent her. It wasn't supposed to be the point of the conference, but someone had an alluring exhibit and a slick way to suck her right in, although that wasn't much of a challenge with Phoebe. Now she is convinced that all that ails her physically, psychically, and professionally can be attributed to the location of her office, the direction of her desk, the lack of a window facing east, and even the scent of her and her co-workers' environment.

A hobby is one thing, but an obsession is another, and Phoebe is a charter member of the obsession-of-the-month club. It is becoming annoying to both her boss and her co-workers because no matter what the subject—performance reviews, project reports, sick days, etc—it is attributed to some mystical cause, rather than personal responsibility and accountability.

Phoebe claims that all will be well again if she can just get an office with a window facing east, and if she can decorate it to the required specifications of her Feng Shui consultant's analysis. Even though her co-workers' workspaces are all wrong too, according to her, she claims she can prevent their ignorance of Feng Shui from affecting her performance if she could just create her own space. She is even willing to pay for it herself—the consultation, the painting, the decorating, the positioning of the furniture, the lighting, etc.

Is this a reasonable request? Is it one that the company should respect? If they do, will that open the door to others wanting to create their own unusual space, and if so, what then?

Analysis

Neither Phoebe nor anyone else has any right to demand re-engineering an organization's workspace, unless there is a safety or hygiene issue or a need to accommodate a disability. Personal opinion as to décor, layout, or any other esoteric aspect of a workplace is the sole purview of the employer.

If Phoebe wants to face east, she can rotate her chair. After all, what if you allow Phoebe to have her way, and then someone else brings in their own personal Feng Shui consultant, and decides that some other arrangement is better, and so on? It's a Pandora's box. Nip it in the bud!

On a more compassionate and even more productive level, some organizations have loosened up considerably about allowing employees to tailor their cubicles or other workspaces in terms of accessories, colors, etc., and some even give employees a decorating allowance to customize their space (within reason). But it does not extend to picking and choosing offices, locations, or other more significant aspects of workspace design and architecture.

Circadian Charlie

Charlie was not like Phoebe. He is not on top of the spiritual or some of the more ephemeral influences on his performance; however, he has proven that, without a doubt, his most creative time of the day (or night) is at 3 a.m. Charlie has more patents and new product and service developments than all his co-workers combined. He is considered a creative genius, albeit strange. His weird brain was always going, but it seemed to go its strongest at 3 a.m. So, what's the problem?

No one disputes the validity of Charlie's creative cycles. In fact, being a progressive and innovative company, they were quite aware that there is such a phenomenon as circadian rhythms that all people have, the timing of which varies from individual to individual. In other words, there are certain times and circumstances in which everyone is more creative, more alert, more effective, etc.

However, because Charlie had identified and mastered his personal circadian cycle, he was actually able to expect and to capitalize upon it each night, resulting in amazing breakthroughs, but causing him to lose sleep and to be essentially useless at the office at 8 a.m. As a result, he tried to schedule mindless activities first thing in the morning, like going through his mail, reading journals, or just reviewing his daily planner. He could not be productive or even attentive at meetings, or work on heavy mental tasks until later in the day. In fact, if it were up to him, he wouldn't even come to work until at least 10 or 11 a.m. at the earliest.

To add even more weirdness to the mix, Charlie had an administrative assistant, Isabel, to whom he would dictate his dreams the following morning. In order to capture the essence of his 3 a.m. brainspurts, Charlie would ask Isabel to "take a letter" while he shared his mental ramblings so he could see them on paper and develop them further. Isabel wasn't bothered by this, and was used to it. In fact, since Charlie was so revered for his breakthroughs and patents, she actually took some pride in being his first sounding board.

After realizing that he could not control his early morning schedule 100%, because others actually preferred early morning staff meetings and projects, Charlie approached his boss about going onto a rather odd form of flextime. His proposal was that on those days in which he had been up at 3 a.m. "creating" that he would not be expected into the office until 10 a.m. so he could catch a couple hours of quality sleep between his brainstorming activity and reporting for work. After all, those two hours between 8 a.m. and 10 a.m. were essentially useless for him anyway!

The interesting challenge here is that Charlie does produce, and his company has great respect for the oddities of a creative culture. Charlie's novel thinking and innovations have benefited the company greatly, and he has a proven track record of results. But how do we accommodate his circadian rhythms and how does one know when he is innovating and when he is sleeping? And what impact will such an accommodation have on his peers' perception of fairness and me-too-ism? Is there a solution that will allow Charlie to continue innovating while not having negative unintended consequences elsewhere?

Analysis

There are several options one could consider in this case, depending upon personal bias and the organization's culture. As usual, there are no hard and fast rules about these types of accommodations. However, given the fact that Charlie is in the category of high-performance weirdos who make significant contributions to the organization, it would probably behoove you to find a way to give a little on this one. On the Behavioral Change Map, the cost-benefit is pretty clear.

At one end of the spectrum, in a pure pay-for-performance organization that can clearly measure results, one would find it very easy to accommodate Charlie, regardless of the hours. For example, sales people on a straight commission might work very different hours and days, and even locations, but as long as they are selling, the company is happy and the employee is happy. No sales, no pay! Lots of sales, lots of pay! Sleep anytime you want to!

Short of that, another option would be to reconsider Charlie's employment status, and to consider making him an independent contractor, which would allow him to work whenever and wherever he wants, as long as he meets the objective(s) in his contract. There are plusses and minuses to both parties in this situation, which would need to be discussed and agreed upon, such as eligibility for benefits, tax implications, etc.

Finally, flextime might be an option, but with a twist. Most flextime programs assume certain "core" hours, and that the employee's hours, whenever they are, are spent *on* the employer's premises. But given Charlie's needs, a hybrid between flextime and telecommuting might fit the bill better. One of the real challenges with Charlie's situation is that he may not be able to tell you which days of the week he will be "creating" at 3 a.m., so trust is obviously a big issue. But again, with his track record, and with expected results clearly identified, it need not be an issue.

And as far as the potential impact on others, unless and until they produce as much as Charlie does, they can just get over it. That's life in a high-performance organization.

What's IN
with High
Performers?

Chapter 3

WHAT'S IN WITH HIGH PERFORMERS?

Initiatives for Creating a High-Performance Organization in the Age of the Individual

As was stated at the outset, organizations must make distinctions as to whether people's behavior is rooted in high performance/high intellect or if they are just being annoying. An additional strategy is to learn how to design organizations around the common needs and values of high performers in general. This is where we should be directing and dedicating more of our time, money, and other resources.

If you do this, the problem, in many cases, will take care of itself because your culture will not only recognize and reward performance over just plain weirdness, but will also learn to accept a certain amount of weirdness as a natural by-product of genius and/or high performance. It will become somewhat of a Darwinian environment, in which the "fittest" are the high performing individuals, and the others will die of natural causes. Figuratively speaking, of course!

The five common needs of high performers are not only interrelated, but also cause and effect. In other words, the first IN, which is

105

INdividualism, weaves through the other four INs. And if you are successful at satisfying the first four INs, the last IN (INnovation) will be a natural outcome: cause and effect. Individuality is the basis, and innovation is the outcome. All the others are means.

In other words, INnovation is a result of an organization's ability to foster and maximize INdividualism, INdependence, INformation, and INcentives. And the need for INdependence, INformation, INcentives, and INnovation are all rooted in the need for INdividualism. See the connection?

As you go through this primer on the specific needs of high performers, think about your own needs and whether you could be achieving greater job and personal success and satisfaction in such an environment. I think you will find that these characteristics, or initiatives, are ultimately universal and not just relevant to geniuses and rare talent. That's the epiphany.

Within each of the five needs, there will be five initiatives necessary to satisfy that need. Let's start with the first, and most fundamental characteristic, and the basis for this book, INdividualism.

INdividualism

1) *High performers can be and want to be weird.*

Hopefully, if you have read this far, you already know that the term "weirdo" is not a pejorative one. It can be a compliment or even a goal—again, if it is rooted in genius or high performance. So it should be obvious why high performers seek out environments in which they can be themselves, and therefore be their best. No one wants to live two lives, one person at work and a different person off the job, but that is exactly what many organizations force people to do. Why else would the majority of people who die at work die on a Monday?

One of the best ways for an organization to adopt a philosophy of individualism is to hire as many different types of individuals as it can. This concept does not just relate to how people look, but how they perform, how they think, how they interact, and how they solve problems. A culture that values and fosters individualism is one that maximizes creative genius as well.

As was mentioned in Chapter 1, traditionalists and bureaucrats like to use the term diversity, but high-performers' concept of diversity, has nothing to do with race, sex, religion, national origin, etc. That is why the term individualism is most central to understanding high performers for what each brings to the game, regardless of the legal or regulatory definitions of diversity.

One way to accomplish and demonstrate this philosophy and to meet this need is to take an inventory of the various talents, skills, and interests (job-related or non-job-related) of each worker so that the organization can tap the full value of each person, and so each worker can be more fulfilled at the same time, which leads to the next initiative.

2) High performers know their strengths and play them to the max.

This initiative goes to the very core of what makes one weirdo a high performer and another one just a weirdo. A common characteristic of highly successful people is that they know their strength(s); they know what they do best and what they love at the same time. They have found the intersection of their *Abilities*, their *Interests*, and the *Market*, which should be the ultimate goal of anyone who wants to strive and thrive in the Age of the Individual. (We will cover this in more detail in Chapter 4, AIM to Be Weird.)

The downside to this accomplishment is that the individuals who are tapping their natural weirdness to the max may fail to see, or even care, how others perceive them. Remember the concept of low self-monitoring discussed in Chapter 1? When someone's strengths become so exaggerated that they overshadow their self-awareness or social skills, they may get labeled as a weirdo (or a pain) by those who don't understand it.

For example, one who is strongly analytical and detail oriented may be a cracker-jack engineer, scientist, or analyst, but when left unchecked may become rigid and agonizingly slow at decision-making because he does not want to make a bad decision (defined as a quick decision) and is very uncomfortable taking what he perceives is an unnecessary risk without having all the facts. Quality above quantity is his motto.

On the other hand, someone else may be highly adept at relationship building, interaction and social skills, and be a whiz-bang sales person or counselor. But taken to the extreme, this same individual can be highly sensitive and emotional and be perfectly comfortable making decisions based more on gut and intuition than on logic and fact. Almost opposite of the person in the prior example!

Neither is wrong! Both are weird! Both are needed. Both have value. But when put together, they can be like oil and water. That is why, in a culture that values individuality, we must also make everyone aware of the divergent behaviors and styles, and help them to see and understand their combined value to the organization. Individuality without tolerance or appreciation creates chaos, stress, and oppression. Judgmentalism without self-reflection creates prima donnas, bigotry, and hypocrisy.

So, to maximize individuality, organizations must not only hire lots of different types, but they must also create an environment that maximizes their strengths and simultaneously educates the masses on the value of these differences and the potential conflicts inherent in such a super-charged workforce. It can be an incredibly powerful force, either positive or negative.

3) *High performers need workplace flexibility.*

The most common flexible workplace initiatives have tended to take the form of flex-time, flex-benefits and even flex-place (i.e., telecommuting), and these are valuable benefits that do enhance an organization's ability to attract, retain, and motivate today's worker. However, taking this concept to the next level to become a *truly* flexible organization requires another dimension, which incorporates the whole person—beyond the job.

For example, a "whole person" who uses his or her technical skills all day may need to "flex" her other, more creative or expressive skills elsewhere. If she cannot find an outlet to use her whole brain on the job, she will be forced to find suitable outlets off the job. Today's worker is not willing to turn off half his brain for half his life.

In the old days, having a second job was called "moonlighting" because it was considered taboo by employers, and it had to be done in the dark of night. It was also done for purely financial reasons—not for self-fulfillment. Today it is called a "composite career" and can be driven more by a need to stimulate mental health, balance, self-worth and fulfillment, and it should be acceptable as long as it does not detract from employees' performance on their "real" jobs.

Today's composite careers don't even need to be paying jobs. An accountant may act in the theatre on weekends; an engineer may volunteer at a local charity; a sales rep may play a competitive sport; a consultant may write books! Whether it is an occupation or an avocation doesn't matter, but it is important to the INdividual that they have the option and the flexibility to pursue either.

In the extreme, this is what led to the advent of sabbaticals and leaves of absence for certain highly stressed, highly skilled employees after a certain period of time in order to regroup, re-charge, and return with a renewed sense of purpose and drive. But the flexibility issue need not even go to these extremes. It can just be a matter of organizational culture and values, which leads to the next initiative.

4) *High performers respect substance over style.*

This is where things can get a little sticky. Obviously, if you hire employees who must interact and develop relationships with the outside world, it is a core requirement of the job that they be presentable. And substance over style does not just refer to personal style or appearance (ref: Blue Suit Bob and Al Naturale), but as much to their modus operandi.

For example, as we now know, everyone has his own personal cycles (Circadian Charlie) resulting in one person being a morning person, someone else being a night person, etc. These rhythms can even extend beyond a daily high/low, to days of the week, and even seasons. But no organization should be expected to be in tune to that degree of INdividuality. Let's be realistic!

Respecting substance over style does not just equate to the end justifying the means. It equates to respecting the fact that some people would rather start with the analysis, move to alternative solutions, seek second opinions, go off and brainstorm in isolation, develop recommendations, etc., in different sequence and in different time frames and with different approaches. It doesn't matter! If the final product is a great one, I don't care if they did it naked, standing on their head while chanting a mantra!

Let me share a personal case study to better demonstrate this concept. In my earlier career, I remember receiving a performance evaluation that rated my "objective" performance measures (i.e., attendance, meeting objectives, communication skills, quality of work, quantity of work, etc.) as distinguished, but resulted in an overall rating as marginal. When I asked how this added up, I was told that it was more a matter of style.

Here I was, a creative type working in a dominantly analytical organization, and my superiors (I use this term loosely) were "uncomfortable" with me because they didn't understand my process of decision making or implementation. Their perception and resultant criticism was that I "shot from the hip" because I did not share all of my analysis and rationale and every possible alternative before proceeding with a recommendation and before moving to implementation. The more important measure or question should have been "Does he hit the target?" Sharpshooters don't have to aim forever! Nor do they need to explain how they do it, as long as they hit the target!

While I am on this tirade, let me share another example that demonstrates the concept of style over substance because this initiative does require examples. After a successful five-year stint at a manufacturing plant, I was promoted to the corporate headquarters of this large, Fortune 100 corporation at a young age because I got results! In fact, I was one of the youngest to ever be promoted to such a position at such an age.

In my first week in the ivory tower, I was on my way to the men's room. Not a difficult task. Approaching me in the hallway was a senior vice president who welcomed me and asked me where I was going. I said, "to the men's room" to which he responded, "Let me give you some advice." A bit strange, I thought, since I had done this many times before and never had a problem meeting my objective, but I am always open to mentoring.

He said, "Whenever you are walking the halls of the corporate headquarters, it would behoove you to have something in your hand." I thought, "hmmm, I will in a few minutes!" but I didn't say it. He proceeded to explain to me that having a piece of paper or a folder or something in your hand makes you "look" like you are walking with a purpose.

I had a purpose! It just wasn't evident at that moment, and it wasn't in my hand (yet!). That interaction stuck with me for a long time (obviously) because it communicated volumes about what was really important to succeed in this environment. Combine that with the "shoot from the hip" scenario, and that is style over substance squared!

5) *High performers need and value their personal space.*

In the world of cubicles and open workplaces, personal space has become a valuable commodity. If you expect high performers to spend the majority of their waking hours "performing," you must also think about their performance habitat. Working from home is an obvious solution, but that is not always possible, nor practical.

Traditionally, and sadly still, many organizations want to prescribe what every square inch of the building is going to look like, including that little corner of the world in which one must live and work. I remember a corporate facility in which no one could bring in a live plant for their office or workspace without it first being inspected, approved, and then quarantined for a period of time to ensure that it would not detract from or harm the corporate flora. This same organization had corporate artwork. Now, this is not a problem if we are talking about the conference room, the hallways, the reception area and the majority of the facility that is common area or visible to the public. But it need not extend to things as simple and as innocuous as photos, knick-knacks, color schemes, or even lighting.

Similar to the concept of Circadian Rhythms, some people do not like bright lights and others do. Ever hear of a dimmer switch? Some people work better with background music, and others are distracted by it. Ever hear of a personal stereo or headphones? Some people like humorous screensavers, in good taste, and some prefer tranquil scenery. Some people like bright colors, others like earth tones, yada yada yada.

On a more serious note, from an ergonomic perspective, some people have a real need for a certain type of chair or computer monitor or wrist pad, etc. If everything is corporately prescribed, you will have to hire clones or build robots, and both are boring. What is more important, performance and morale, or homogeneity and control? Give them liberty, or give them to the competition.

INdependence

1) High performers place great value on their freedoms.

There is a very important reason why INdependence comes next. It is not only a natural outgrowth of individuality, but it also supports and weaves through all the other needs, ultimately building to the last initiative, which is INnovation. Keep this in the back of your mind so that by the time you get to the end of this section, it will all come together into a glorious "A-HA!"

To speak of independence as a workplace concept would have been unheard of in the early days of the Industrial-era society, when people were hired primarily to carry out a task and were given as little discretion as possible. That was called Scientific Management. That was the Age of the Organization Man. Create the "perfect system" so that people could not possibly screw up, so that "management" required nothing more than giving orders.

Today, we have evolved to hiring brains over brawn, to valuing the mind over muscle. In fact, a common phrase in the good old days was to "check your brain at the door" and just do what you are told. But, in the "new normal," the demand is for diversity, differentiation, creativity, and innovation.

How things have changed! Or have they? Times may have changed, but most organizational models have not kept pace with the needs and demands of today's markets or today's talent. We are trying to force square pegs into round holes, then cannot figure out why these new workers cannot succeed. We've got new workers in an old model.

The fact that high performers place great value on their freedoms extends to everything in their lives, personally and professionally, which will become clearer as we put the five initiatives of INdependence together.

2) *High performers resist bureaucracy.*

Patience is *not* a high performer's virtue, particularly when it comes to getting things done at work, and particularly when he or she does not have control over the processes to do so. Remember the discussion about self-efficacy in Chapter 1? If you want to run the best and brightest out the door in a hurry, make it a monumental task to order staples. Create a committee for everything.

High performers must be trusted and must have the INdependence to get things done without a lot of red tape. The word *trust* is key here. There is an inverse relationship between the amount of trust in an organization and the number of policies and procedures in effect. In other words, the less trust, the more bureaucracy.

Remember System Tester Sam? He was a perfect example of this value and need in action. "If I have to write numerous, redundant reports on 'how I spent my last five days, four weeks, or three months,' then you must not trust me and you are also putting bureaucracy in the way of my getting my real job done."

The word policy has its roots in the Greek word, "polis." Guess what other word is rooted in "polis?" That's right! Police! High performers do not want nor need to be policed by their organizations. If you do not trust them to do the right thing, then you hired the wrong person to begin with—which leads to the next initiative, which is a logical offshoot of the first two.

3) *High performers can be difficult to manage.*

If you hired the right person in the first place, they should not need to be "managed."

Is that idealistic? Not if you understand what the word manage really means. The Latin root of the word manage is "manus" which means "hand" or "to handle." High performers do not want or need to be handled.

It is important to make a distinction here between the concepts of management and leadership. High performers love leaders, but they must be charismatic leaders. A charismatic leader leads people the way they want to be led, not the way he or she wants to lead them. That means that the leader has a keen appreciation for and understanding of the exact principles we are highlighting here, and then taps them for mutual value and benefit.

So, don't *handle* high-performers; *lead* them!

4) *High performers are goal-oriented.*

How does being goal-oriented relate to INdependence? Give high-performers a goal, set them loose, and get out of the way. Don't prescribe exactly how a creative or mental challenge is to be accomplished. Prescribed creativity is an oxymoron!

High performers focus on ends more than means. Their philosophy is that as long as they do nothing illegal, immoral, or unethical, you should leave them alone to get to the goal. Given that there is almost always more than one right answer in today's professional workplace, you may suggest your ideas and alternatives, but do not prescribe them. Leaders envision and set goals; managers "handle." Be a leader!

Can you see how this initiative relates to the need for flexibility? If not, you will. Whether one does his or her work at 3 a.m. or 3 p.m. shouldn't matter (see Circadian Charlie). Everyone has his or her own body clock, and some people are more creative in the morning and some at night. Thus the need for flex-time, but a new generation of flextime—no time clock at all! Just results!

You will also see how this initiative relates to the later concept of INcentives because high performers want to be measured and rewarded on their results (i.e., goal accomplishment), not how they got there. Are you starting to see the relationships?

5) *High performers must be self-directed.*

This initiative is very closely related to principal #4, that high-performers are goal-oriented. However, this one relates to the "need" for high-performers to be motivated from within, or intrinsically. Although it is rather idealistic for anyone to expect that every task must be exciting and sexy, whoever said high performers were realistic? It isn't unrealistic,

> *You can tame a fanatic, but you can't breathe life into a corpse!*

however, for managers and leaders to understand that high performers, in the long run, are most motivated by tasks and environments that make them *want* to perform versus *have* to perform.

Even the less sexy tasks will be tackled with more vigor if the high performer can see the value in the task. In order to make any assignment more satisfying the following five core characteristics must be maximized:[1]

Skill Variety: The degree to which a job requires a variety of different activities in carrying out the work assignment and involves the use of a number of different skills and talents of the employee.

Task Identity: The degree to which the job requires completion of a whole identifiable piece of work—that is, one that involves doing a job from beginning to end with a visible outcome.

Task Significance: The degree to which the job is perceived as important and involves a meaningful contribution to the organization or society in general.

---

1. J. R. Hackman & G. R. Oldham, *The Relationship Among Core Job Dimensions, the Critical Psychological States, and On-the-job Outcomes*, The Job Diagnostic Survey: An Instrument for the Diagnosis of Jobs and the Evaluation of Job Redesign Projects, Yale University, (1974), 3.
Alternative Source: J.R. Hackman & G.R. Oldham, "Development of the Job Diagnostic Survey," *Journal of Applied Psychology,* April 1975, pp. 159–70.

Autonomy: The degree to which the job gives the employee substantial freedom, independence, and discretion in scheduling the work and determining procedures used in carrying it out.

Feedback: The degree to which carrying out the work activities results in the employee obtaining direct and clear information on how well the job has been done.

INformation

1) *High performers want to get their information from the source.*

There's that "trust" concept again! Studies show that the number one source of "trusted" information in most organizations is the grapevine. The grapevine isn't sugar-coated. It comes from people that employees think they can trust, and it is easily accessible. Wouldn't if be nice if the formal information sources could boast these same qualities? Well, they can!

Research shows that employees would *prefer* to get their information from the source, meaning the leadership and its communication vehicles, but distrust of the source prevents that from happening. The most effective measure an organization can take to overcome this barrier is to adopt an "open book management" philosophy. In other words, expand information sharing from a "need to know" to a "want to know" basis.

Again, if you cannot trust your people with information, you've not only hired the wrong people, but you cannot progress through these initiatives. Trust is the enemy of bureaucracy but is communication's greatest ally.

Again, are you seeing the common threads?

2) *High performers have a need to know and a need to let know.*

Just as high performers would like to get the truth from formal, official channels, they would also like to be able to tell the leadership their version of the truth. One-way communication is telling. Two-way communication is liberating.

Some may call them prima donnas, but high performers do sometimes think they know it all. Even if they *don't* know it all, they probably know something you don't, and vice versa. Even more important, they may know something that you *should* know, but don't! Look at how many of the cases demonstrated that principle! As a manager, you have nothing to lose and everything to gain.

The reason we now have "whistleblower" laws to protect workers who "rat" on their employers is because no one within the organization's so-called leadership wanted to hear it, or if they did hear it, they ignored it, denied it, or even stifled it. That just won't work in a high-performance workplace, or in a society that values its freedoms and rights (i.e., in the Age of Individual).

With all the jargon and programs centered around team-building and quality, it is rather ironic to think that an organization could have either without total two-way disclosure. What successful team do you know of where the players don't know all the plays? What level of quality can you expect from people who don't know as much as possible about what goes into the product or service?

The first step to high-performing organizations is the ability for its members to hear and be heard, without filters and without retribution. If you owned the company, wouldn't you want to know everything? High performers think almost like owners, and anything short of the cold, hard, unvarnished truth is a lie, which leads to the reason for the next initiative:

3) *High performers distrust bureaucratic channels.*

There's that "trust" word again! Traditional company publications have become so sterile and politically correct that few people rely upon them for "the truth." Not that they are lies, but they certainly do not lack for sugar coating. High performers want the good, the bad, and the ugly, and they want it in its raw form. Think of it as "sugar-free candor"! If your fear is that people won't understand or use the information appropriately, then you obviously do not trust them, so their perception *is* reality!

One of the key requirements of open book management is that people be trained on how to read and interpret such things as financials and other documents so that they can be trusted to understand them and to put them into proper perspective. Additionally, even if your people are not as adept as you would like them to be, there is nothing wrong with including an interpretive analysis or executive summary. If the raw information is accurate and candid, then an analysis by top management will be appreciated, rather than suspect.

Another reason why high performers distrust bureaucratic channels of information is that the communiqués are usually written in such a sterile and legalistic manner that most people don't even want to go to the effort to try to cut through and decipher the core message. A solution to this dilemma is to lighten up wherever you can in your day-to-day communication. Not everything must be written by lawyers. Even a little humor is not only appropriate, but refreshing to high performers. Be real!

4) *High performers think conflict can be positive.*

In fact, most high performers even like it! Conflict is essential to creativity, as long as the conflict centers around issues and not people. Depersonalized conflict involves listening to diverse perspectives while withholding judgment so that solutions are much richer and much better received.

High performers are suspicious of too much harmony. Teamwork does not imply total harmony. Total harmony implies a lack of conflict, "me-tooism," excess homogeneity, and a culture of political correctness over creativity. If two people in an organization agree on everything, one of them probably isn't needed. It is the organization that can actually have fun with conflict that fosters and maximizes high performance.

If you are forming a team that is to work on anything involving change, do not fall victim to selecting team members based upon how well they get along and go along. In fact, do just the opposite. Remember System Tester Sam? Creative Dissatisfaction? Put mavericks and malcontents on the team. Then make them put up or shut up!

Appointing mavericks and malcontents to a change team will result in one of two outcomes. They will either tap their creative dissatisfaction and come up with innovative ideas, or they will punch themselves out and come to the painful realization that they are just noisemakers, which will probably squelch them in future situations. Either way, the organization wins!

5) *High performers want the "why" with the "what."*

High performers are not satisfied with being told *what* to do without knowing *why*. They are motivated from within, not just by outside forces. And anyone is more willing to accept and embrace change or challenge if they have a reason. That's just human nature. Without a reason, there is no motivation.

A simple but interesting experiment was done in which people were instructed to try to cut in line to use a photocopier. The first time, they were instructed to merely try to cut in, without giving a reason. They would say, "Excuse me. May I cut in?" And the overwhelming majority of the time, people would abruptly say, "No. Get in line!"

Then the experiment was repeated, but this time the intruder would give a reason. They might say, "Excuse me. Would you mind if I cut in line? I am double-parked." Or, "Excuse me. Would you mind if I cut in line? I am late for a meeting." And in these cases, the over-whelming majority of people said, "Sure, go ahead!"

The reason? The reason! Yes, the reason people were more amena-ble to being inconvenienced, to being flexible, and to deferring to an intruder was that they were given a reason, or a "why." That is the motivation that is required to get someone to do what someone else wants them to do.

Knowledge workers, by their very nature, are motivated by seeing and understanding the bigger picture and by feeling a part of it. It no longer suffices just to tell people what to do. Any type of change, be it personal, organizational, or societal, involves three key components: The *what*, the *how*, and the *why*. Traditionally, managers would sit in a room and discuss *what* has to be done. That's the knowledge. Then, they would announce to the implementers (workers) their decision. "We must do X!"

The next logical question from the workers and implementers was, "How are we going to get there or do that?" The *how* is the means, which would result in some type of training, process brainwashing, or introduction of some new-fangled tool or technique. Ultimately, when the change failed to take hold or was resisted, the reason was usually rooted in the *why*, which is the motivation.

To sum up: *What* is the knowledge; *how* is the means; *why* is the motivation.

No one ever thought to get buy-in up front from those responsible for embracing and implementing the change by involving them in the reasons or rationale for it. If management doesn't initiate change for no reason, why would we expect employees to be any different? It isn't even their idea!

In the Age of the Individual, this model must be turned upside down. Ideally, astute managers and leaders must facilitate workers to self-discovery as to the "why" for new initiatives. When people can draw their own conclusions, and reach their own "Aha's!" the motivation is natural; it is intrinsic; it is powerful; it is exactly the kind of motivation high performers need to excel. Then *they* will actually *ask* for the "how"—the tools and techniques and training to make it happen. You don't have to sell it to them or ram it down their throats!

The most common management objection to this approach is that it just takes too much time. Yes, it may take more time and effort up front, but why is it that there is never enough time to do a project right the first time and make it stick, but there is always enough time to do it over? It is this mentality that keeps snake oil consultants fat and happy!

If, for some reason, self-discovery is not possible or feasible, the second-best route is to begin the announcement process with the "why" instead of the "what" and to share the logic and conclusion first. Once you share the "why" it is easier for people to buy the "what" if it makes sense to them. Again, high performers and knowledge workers want and need you to respect their ability to be able to process bigger picture information rather than to just have the outcomes dictated to them. If it's worth doing, it's worth doing right!

INcentives

1) *High performers are not afraid of pay for performance.*

All workers are not created equal. It's amazing how many managers and organizational leaders lament that pay has lost its impact as a motivator. It is true! And they are to blame because the average differential in pay between a mediocre performer and a superior performer in the same job, in the same company, is only about 3–5%. Of course pay is not a motivator!

But it doesn't have to be that way. It is only because weak managers have lacked the creativity and/or the backbone to implement *real* pay-for-performance programs. A paycheck is like breathing....you take it for granted until it stops. It has become an expectation, not a catalyst for achieving great things. High performers are not afraid of pay for performance, and in fact, they demand it!

> *A paycheck is like breathing... you take it for granted until it stops!*

Another fallacy of traditional managers is that pay-for-performance means spending more money. I find it sadly ironic when I hear a manager say, "We cannot afford a pay-for-performance program." You cannot afford performance? Isn't that where the money ultimately comes from in order to pay people in the first place?

Pay for performance does not mean spending more money. It means allocating it differently. You can take the same 5% "merit" budget and rather than giving one person 4% and another 6% to average out to an overall 5%, you give your top performer 10% and your worst loser nothing! That's still an overall average of 5%, and yes, it is legal! It is not only legal, but it is moral! That's a meritocracy! (A meritocracy is an organization in which one's success or failure is tied directly to his or her personal contribution or performance.)

In a meritocracy and in the Age of the Individual, *fair is not equal*! Human resources professionals and managers in general have become so hypersensitized to the concept of "equality" that they think and operate under the misguided belief that everyone must be treated the same. As a result, they are pushing everyone's performance down to an "equal" level of mediocrity.

If the average pay differential between a high performer and an average performer is a mere 3 to 5%, you are effectively rewarding the average performer and punishing the high performer! That's the Law of Unintended Consequences. In your quest to be fair, you end up being unfair and ineffective! No wonder you can't afford pay for performance. And guess who ends up leaving the organization? Yes, the winners—thus making you a loser too. In this scenario, the only winners are the losers!

It is interesting to hear what some managers have to say about increasing discrimination in pay. "If I give 10% to Joe and nothing to Mary, Mary is going to be de-motivated!" She is already de-motivated! That is why she is not being rewarded! Tell her why Joe got 10% and why she got nothing! That's how you earn your pay and title as a manager! And then tell her how she can succeed and what she needs to do to get a "merit" raise next time. Help her to succeed, but don't help everyone else to fail.

Another salient quote I hear is, "But if I don't give Fred a reasonable raise, he might leave!" Hooray! No unemployment compensation! No wrongful discharge lawsuit! In addition to the fallacy that "equal is fair" is the fallacy that turnover is always bad. Some turnover can be good! If you are losing the losers and winning the winners, it is positive turnover. You are now on the road to successfully creating a culture of performance that will not tolerate mediocrity, and the rewards for that are astounding, for both the employee and the employer. It becomes self-fulfilling.

2) *High performers respond well to nontraditional incentives.*

Whether you use the word incentives, or rewards, or recognition, there is almost no limit to the ways in which high performers can be motivated, and they are not limited to things financial. In fact, from a business and motivation perspective, it is better that performance incentives *not* be closely linked to the traditional compensation program. We've already discussed the concept of *pay* for performance in the prior section, so now let's talk about the other types of *rewards* or incentives.

> ***That which is observed, measured, and rewarded gets done***

High performers need to be stroked. But it must be genuine, and from an organizational management perspective, it must be deserved. But because high performers respect creativity, they appreciate "out-of-the-box" types of rewards, regardless of monetary value. In the performance improvement business, this is called "trophy value."

Think about how people cherish trophies. Most of us still have trophies or certificates of achievement of some type in our attic or basement for accomplishments many years ago. We will never throw them away! Now think about the actual monetary value of a trophy. It's essentially worthless! Most are made of the cheapest materials money can buy and have no utilitarian value at all. You can't eat them, you can't wear them, you can't sell them, you can't even use them for much of anything besides a doorstop or a paperweight. But they are priceless in the mind of the recipient.

Moral of the story? It ain't the money, honey! It's what it stands for that matters, i.e., trophy value. The same is true of organizational performance incentives. Money is always nice, but trophies tend to have more lasting value and greater impact. Organizational trophies can come in many forms, such as employee of the month awards, pins, coffee mugs, plaques for attaining goals, certificates, or even an actual trophy that rotates from department to department or person to person depending on who the current "winner" is (sales leader, perfect attendance, best new idea, etc.) for that month or quarter.

In my first book, *Get Weird!* there was even an idea called "Name That Room" in which companies named various conference rooms, hallways, and the like, in honor of individuals, customers, or others who are deserving of special recognition. Again, the variations are limitless. Even if your company has not adopted a true pay-for-performance system, these nontraditional incentives can go a long way to fill the void. Plus, they can be varied and kept fresh and fun depending on current organizational needs and goals. And high performers love them!

3) *High performers resent low-performers.*

This one is probably self-evident. But it bears explaining because high performers won't sit around and wait for dead wood to be discarded or revived. If you are effective in initiatives #1 and #2 (i.e., pay for performance and non traditional incentives) this one may take care of itself. But the bottom line is that high performers want to work in a culture of high performance, and it is incongruent to keep people forever who do not produce or who detract from the success of others.

Tolerating low performance is not just a matter of internal equity. It is symbolic of other, larger issues, none of which will keep high performers flourishing within your organization. Allowing non-performers or low performers to suck the resources out of the organization is symbolic of weak management and weak values, and high performers need to respect those who are supposed to be their leaders.

Admittedly, high performers do have a tendency to see everyone else as dead wood. This is another manifestation of their prima donnaish behavior. The ultimate solution to both issues, weeding out non/low performers and ensuring objectivity, is to make performance measures clear, to communicate their attainment or lack thereof on a regular basis, and to link them to compensation and incentives as directly and immediately as possible. Then there is no question as to how people are doing, and why they are being rewarded, or not!

4) *High performers want a reason to work hard.*

The key word here is "want," not "need." The work ethic is dead. Get over it! Organizations no longer have the luxury of being able to hire people with little or no art, science, or sophistication in the selection process, or to expect them to just do what they are told and to keep coming back for more forever. This is particularly true for high-performance workers.

During my graduate work, there were two distinctly separate but simultaneous research studies going on that demonstrated this very well. On the one side, the Public Agenda Foundation had determined that only 22% of working Americans admitted to working at their full potential. On the other hand, Gallup had conducted a survey that determined that 88% of working Americans *wanted* to perform at their full potential at work. Is that contradictory? No!

What these dichotomous studies demonstrated, albeit without either of them knowing it at the time, was the concept of "Discretionary Effort": Potential minus Performance = Discretionary Effort. Discretionary effort is that performance which employees keep bottled up inside them, or in their hip pockets, because they do not see a reason or a need to use it. It is the difference between doing just enough to get by, i.e., mediocrity, versus accomplishing great things, i.e., a meritocracy.

Why do they hold back and keep some discretionary effort to themselves? Because the rewards do not elicit it, the mission does not foster it, and the leadership does not instill it. All the things that are embodied in the five needs of high performers are lacking.

By their very nature, high performers are looking for work that taps their natural talents and abilities. (See "AIM" in Chapter 4.) That is what gets them out of bed in the morning (or at night), to follow a passion. Not all work must be a calling, but it must be intrinsically motivating.

This initiative is somewhat related to the need to know the "why" with the "what" in the section on INformation. Remember, as was mentioned at the outset, that all these needs and initiatives are tightly inter-twined. Seeing the bigger picture, being a part of it, understanding one's critical value, being recognized for it, etc., are all contributing factors to creating an environment in which people perform because they want to, not just because the have to. Do you see it coming together?

5) *High performers love to celebrate.*

And often! Now that we know that the work ethic is dead, we are ready to come to the realization that work and fun need not be opposites. Another blasphemy! What is this world coming to? If you look up the word "work" in Webster's Dictionary you will find synonyms like "labor, travail, toil, drudgery, grind," none of which get me jumping out of bed in the morning.

But is it realistic to think that work should be fun? Maybe not. But it need not be constant labor, travail, toil, drudgery, or grind either! Even if the tasks at hand are not exactly fun, they can be fulfilling (see the characteristics of an enriched job on page 116). And even if not everything can be fulfilling, we can still celebrate accomplishments, either individually or organizationally. And that is what high performers both want and need in order to keep going at a pace that taps their discretionary effort.

Work is not work to high performers. It may not be a calling, but they would at least like it to be more than just work. And that is not only possible, but necessary. High performers also love and appreciate spontaneous fun. It need not be a big, annual company picnic. In fact, it is better if it is "on the spot" fun. Some of the best times are not planned.

There are numerous examples of creative, inexpensive, and effective ways to have fun detailed in my first book, *Get Weird! 101 Innovative Ways to Make Your Company a Great Place to Work.* Things like "One Minute Parades" where co-workers march around someone's cubicle to draw attention to a special milestone or accomplishment, or

"Peer Pats" where people can tangibly recognize each other spontaneously, and many more.

The CEO of one of my clients arranged to bring in a dance instructor at lunchtime so everyone could learn the latest dance craze within an hour. He had sandwiches and beverages delivered, routed the phones, and for an hour the place went nuts (in a good way!). It's these types of quick, easy, inexpensive, and spontaneous activities that begin to create a culture of fun, rather than to rely solely on the same old events that become as much of a chore as a celebration. Here's a hint.... Lunch with the boss ain't no prize!

Many high performers have adopted the lifestyle motto: "Work hard, play hard!" and understand that each aspect of life supports the other. Some may live to work, but even those who just work to live still want to enjoy their life at work. High-performers admire and value the creativity of incremental celebrations and fun-on-the-fly, which results in work and pleasure coming together as one. How can anyone argue with that?

INnovation

REMINDER

Everything up to this point is a contributor to INnovation. As we've clearly established, these needs and their respective initiatives have strong overlap and cause and effect. So, the more INdividualism, INdependence, INformation, and INcentives you have, the more INnovation will result.

1) *High performers are not afraid of, but crave new technology.*

Admittedly, this one is not a universal truth, but it is more the case than not. If not new technology, at least new thinking and approaches to problem solving are of great value. It is just as important to know that those who must attempt to manage or lead high performers need not have that same craving, as long as they make it available to their workers.

A common pitfall of managers of high performers, and especially managers of technology workers, is the misguided assumption that they have to pretend they have the same or higher level of interest and understanding of current trends and tools and technology. It would be nice, yes. But it stands to reason that younger, more currently educated employees will come to the game with more cutting edge knowledge and skills, and the desire to maintain them.

> *If smart managers always hire people smarter than themselves, wouldn't that mean that the dumbest people are at the top?*

And nothing will burn a manager faster than trying to fake his or her way through this one. This is an opportunity to build credibility by admitting your fallibility. High performers relish the thought that they know more than you do, and they respect managers who aren't afraid to admit it. Managers do not need to know more than their underlings about the technical aspects of their work. Again, it would be nice, but it isn't essential as long as you can *trust* that they are getting the job done. Remember trust? Remember substance over style?

So, once you get past the ego issue, the next step is to make new learning and tools available to the greatest extent possible, but obviously based on cost-benefit, unless it is merely a perk or performance reward. Beware that the really high-tech, high-performance worker can behave like a junkie and may insist that he or she needs the newest and most expensive gadgets and toys all the time just to survive. This is a fallacy and is nonsensical from a business perspective unless you have unlimited resources or you use toys as a substitute for bonuses or other rewards. What they really want is 1) to be able to play with them, and 2) to show them off to their friends and colleagues who don't have them yet.

Just as a footnote, also beware that you, the manager, should not be the first one to get the latest and greatest gizmo if you aren't truly going to use it more than your workers would. Years ago, when the first personal computers hit the scene, it was a sad state of affairs to see that the Organization Men had them collecting dust on their desks because they were perks and status symbols.

In the meantime, their secretaries, who were totally responsible for word processing, bookkeeping, record keeping, etc., continued to beat the keys off an old typewriter, making corrections with White-out, while begging and drooling for the exact technology their bosses had on their desks and couldn't even turn on.

2) *High performers must be free to risk, stretch, and err.*

With increased INnovation comes the increased likelihood of risk and error. Honest error. Well-intentioned error. But error, nonetheless. And to make it work to the advantage of the organization, it must be responded to in a certain way.

Success comes from good judgment, good judgment comes from experience, and experience comes from bad judgment

Another story. One of the most exciting, high performance and creative environments I have ever experienced was early in my career when, during my new employee orientation, I was introduced to my boss's boss, who said, "John, welcome to XYZ! I expect you to screw up!" I thought he must have checked my references and began to panic. (Just kidding!)

But he followed up by saying, "You have a great education and we are paying you a good salary. We expect you to stretch, to try new things, and in the process you are going to make some mistakes. If you never make any mistakes, I have to assume you are just maintaining the status quo and not trying anything new, and we can find someone with a lot less education and for a lot less money who can do that."

He wrapped up his orientation lecture by saying, "I have only three rules regarding this issue. They are, 1) that the mistake was a well-intentioned and honest one. In other words, you weren't deliberately trying to screw up the company; 2) that you learn from it and never make the same mistake twice; and 3) that you come to me and let me know about it before I have to find out about it from someone else. My promise to you is that if you meet those three rules, you will never be punished or fired for it."

I think that story pretty well sums it up. High performers, when given the latitude and trust to be creative and innovative do not abuse the privilege. In fact, just the opposite occurs. They value and cherish this environment so much that they will do everything in their power to use the privilege to excel and to produce incredible results. But, as we know, that doesn't mean that they are easy to manage, which leads to the next initiative.

3) *High performers like to initiate change and rock the boat.*

Granted, some of the challenges of high performers can actually be exacerbated by granting them all the things that are being advocated here, like INdependence, INformation, etc. Because, for example, the more information they have, the more ability they will have to question and criticize. The more INcentives there are, the more they will analyze the criteria and equity of them, and so on.

So, is the solution to just throw this book away and go back to the ease of the autocracy? Of course not! But you can if you want, because you already paid for it. High performers can become quite arrogant and start to think they know more or better about everything. Let them! Make them put their superiority complex to good use!

Whenever a high performer starts to get cranky about a particular policy, procedure, or other workplace demand or distraction over which they may not have any legitimate involvement or control (or even if they do), just turn it around. Remember System Tester Sam and "Creative Dissatisfaction"? Rather than shooting them down at the knees, say "Hmm. Very interesting. What's your idea for improvement? Can you put together a cost-benefit proposal for me and show me the alternatives and why they are better? We're always looking for new ideas!"

You don't have to shoot them and/or their ego down. It may feel good, but that will only backfire on you. Calmly validate their perspective, then redirect it toward employee-driven solutions.

Bottom line, when you are hiring the best and the brightest and setting them free, you can expect some conflict. And conflict is essential to creativity and INnovation. Just lead by example and be sure to show your people how you depersonalize conflict and attack processes and not people, issues and not individuals, and you can't go wrong— nor can you go back to the way you've always done things.

4) *High performers are most creative when they are loose.*

When do you get brainspurts? These are little brainstorms that just pop into your head when you least expect them. Most people answer this question with, in the car, in the shower, while jogging, working in the garden, in bed, etc. It's almost never at work! How sad. Which is exactly the point. Creative juices flow when you are loose, when you aren't trying, when you are relaxed.

This initiative is actually one that is the most impacted by satisfaction of some of the others. The more my INdividuality is respected and fostered and the more INformation I have, and the more INdependence I am allowed, the more relaxed I will be, and thus the more free-flowing my mind can and will be. It's very similar to the dynamics of a free-agent mentality.

This is exactly why most of the significant inventions and break-throughs in modern history rarely occur in large corporate or academic research labs, but rather in basements, garages, skunk works—and by accident. There isn't a whole lot more to say about this initiative because it is so highly dependent upon the satisfaction of the others. But once you have created an environment of "looseness," you can really capitalize upon it by facilitating the next initiative.

5) *High performers feed on each others' creative weirdness.*

This component is not unique to high performers, but they do seem to understand and appreciate it more than the average person. If you have ever gone to lunch or to some other informal gathering of high per-formers who are in a similar pro-fession or interest group, you will see it in action. From mind benders to group challenges to weird what-iffing, it can even be a little nerdy, but who cares?

> *If nonconformists only associate with other nonconformists, doesn't that make them conformists?*

History shows that many of the most successful and creative geniuses of our world were pretty nerdy, or nonconformist, or even counter-culture, which is why they feed on each other. High-perform-ing weirdos feel more comfortable and *normal* associating with other so-called weirdos. They are accepted, validated, and even valued.

High performers also like to know there are other high performers in their environs because it boosts their ego, their self-esteem, and their commitment to stay and perform. They want to be able to respect their associates, even if they won't admit it, and even if they constantly act like they are superior to everyone else. It's just part of their schtick.

So, maximize the opportunity by allowing those natural synergies to develop and grow. Just don't blow it by making it a formal program. You can foster this synergy by creating opportunities for nerd camaraderie. This is *not* team-building. *Please* do not call it team-building. These are just opportunities for collaboration, association, or commiseration. This is the Age of the Individual!

If you do plan to use the value of nerd synergy for organizational gain, like on a project or new initiative, restrict the creative feeding frenzy to periodic brainstorming or mind-mapping sessions, but do not impose the "team thing" for an entire project. This initiative has to happen because they want it to, when they want it to, where they want it to, and because it is enjoyable, not because it is required as part of a program. Facilitate; don't dictate!

IN Conclusion

Bottom line: If you wanted to boil all these concepts down to a single formula, it would be this:

Individuality + Freedom = High Performance

In other words, once the value of the "individual" (the weirdness within) is recognized and realized, and the environment is created in which to set it free, the opportunities are limitless for all.

Ironically, the U.S. has more of these two characteristics than any other country in the world, but we fail to capitalize upon them. What other culture has more diversity (individuality) than the U.S.? What other country has more freedom? We have little or no control over the amount of diversity (individuality) that is present in our country or even in most of our organizations. But we do have control over how much freedom we provide within them.

Where do we push the limits, and where do we draw the lines? One enables, the other stifles. That limit is best drawn at the point where the benefit to the greater good stops; the point at which weird-ness crosses over from synergism to narcissism.

Granted, as was demonstrated in many of the case studies, some freedoms cannot go totally unchecked in the workplace, such as pri-vacy, search and seizure, or speech, but there is no business or human resource justification for limiting the creative and productive capabili-ties of the workforce purely out of fear of being different.

Every company talks about "differentiating" itself in the market-place, and every company wants to have a "unique value proposition" and to spew all the other program-of-the-month jargon to pretend they are progressive. But most of these same companies fail to recognize that the only real variable that distinguishes one company from another is the human element.

No matter what you sell—cars, hamburgers, insurance, whatever it is—your product/service is a commodity in the eyes of Joe Consumer. Unless you have a monopoly, the only perceived difference between Company A and Company B is whether I like you and whether it feels good to do business with you, and that boils down to how the product or service is delivered, which is ultimately determined by your employees.

Follow these recipes for "What's IN With High Performers?" and you will create a truly healthy and wonderfully weird culture in which genius and excellence are merely a natural by-product of individuality and freedom coming together with the right structure and process.

Tools and Techniques to Change Others, Organizations, and Yourself

Chapter 4 ————

TOOLS AND TECHNIQUES TO CHANGE OTHERS, ORGANIZATIONS, AND YOURSELF

Behavioral Change Map

Preface

Any behavioral or performance issue can be boiled down to two possi-

> *Most jerks at work are not born, they are created*

ble root causes: motivation or skill. Yes, it's that simple. Unfortunately, isolating and correcting the issue is a different matter. But it really is just a matter of 1) s/he doesn't want to do it, or 2) s/he can't do it. Look at all the cases again, and you will see that this is true.

The flowchart in Figure 4.1 is intended to 1) walk you through the mental exercise of determining which of the two issues, motivation or skill, is at play; 2) tell you why; and then 3) tell you what to do about it.

Behavioral Change Map

A Guide to When and How to Intervene in Any Indivdual Behavioral Challenge

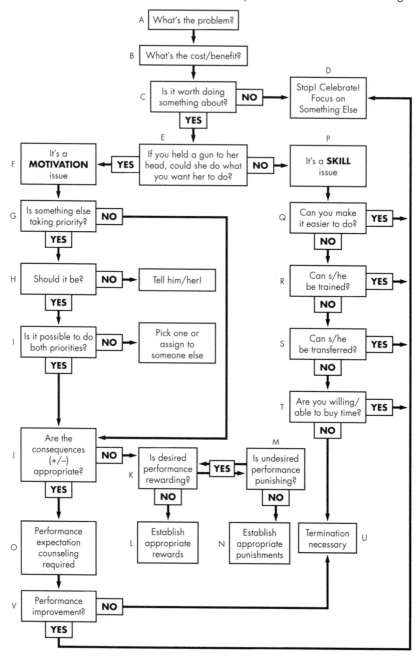

FIGURE 4.1   Behavioral Change Map.

The most important thing a manager can manage is consequences, but that is exactly what many managers tend to sidestep or screw up. Pay for performance, for example, is a form of managing consequences.

As was detailed in the section on INcentives, a good manager *must* discriminate...based upon performance. That is what managing consequences is all about. If something good happens when I do X, I will want to do X again. If I am caused pain or discomfort when I do Y, I will probably avoid doing it again, unless I am a masochist, which is a different book! If nothing happens when I do X or Y I can choose to do whatever I want to do, because it doesn't matter. Can you see how this plays out in the workplace? Can you see how it might also play out at home?

Admit it or not, humans are not that different from other animals in terms of operant conditioning, AKA the Pavlovian Response. Give Fido a cookie when he sits, and he learns that sitting is a good thing and will probably do it again. Give Fido a cookie when he poops on the carpet, and you will quickly learn what happens to bad managers.

You will note that there is a letter code beside each box of the flowchart, so you can follow along with the examples and become more adept at using it for your own behavioral challenges.

A. *What's the problem?*

Although you may think this is obvious, it isn't. In fact, many good intentions can go awry right here by not defining the real problem up front, or not defining it appropriately. Rather than couching the problem or challenge in emotional terms or as a personal irritant, define it as an organizational problem, if it is.

For example, rather than stating the issue as "Tom has a bad attitude," drill down and define what that means. How is his "bad" attitude manifested in the workplace? Is he badmouthing customers? Is he disruptive to others? Is he insubordinate? Or is he just different from you (a weirdo) in a way that bugs you? After all, you can never effectively coach or counsel an employee to improve or change without being able to provide specific examples of the problem.

Let's start with an easy one. The problem is that John leaves for lunch a half hour early each day and his co-workers are complaining to the boss, assuming he is taking longer than allowed lunches every day. The standard lunch hour is noon to 1 p.m.

In reality, John leaves at 11:30 a.m. so he can beat the lunch rush at the local health club to work out, so he is back on the job by 12:30 p.m., so he is not taking more than the prescribed hour for lunch. So, the assumption by John's co-workers that he is taking long lunches is a faulty one to begin with. He has just taken the liberty of going early and returning early, but with good intentions. His co-workers don't know he is back at his desk a half hour early because they're out to lunch! A conundrum?

B. What's the cost/benefit?

Objectively, there is no net loss here since John is doing something healthful and stress reducing, and not taking more time off the job than he would if he went next door and sucked down a couple of burgers and a beer. So, what's the problem? It is costing the company nothing for John to maintain his health and his positive attitude.

C. Is it worth doing something about?

Doubtful! Since John does not have the type of job that requires him to be physically present at prescribed times, such as a 9-1-1 operator, a technical service phone rep, a production worker, or an on-call employee, his leaving at 11:30 a.m. is essentially harmless. At most, if his co-workers have a problem with it, just tell them why he is not there at 11:30 a.m., that he is back a half hour before they are, and that a professional should be able to use his or her judgment as to what is appropriate flexibility. Remember INdividuality and INdependence?

As an aside, however, this issue may also lead you to the conclusion that your strict lunch hour policy may be unnecessarily rigid for a professional work place in which discretion is valued and trust essential. There's that "trust" word again! You may want to revisit your lunch policy so you don't have to deal with such mundane issues in the future.

Bottom line? Go to box "D"

D. Stop! Celebrate! Focus on something else!

Now, let's focus on an issue that may be worth doing something about. See how this works? Back to "A."

A. What's the problem?

Sally is lazy. Not good enough! Be more specific. How is it being demonstrated? Is she falling asleep at her desk? Is she missing deadlines?

Let's assume Sally's typing/word processing accuracy is the issue, for purposes of walking through the flow chart.

B. What's the cost/benefit?

How are Sally's typing/word processing errors affecting the organization? What is it costing?

In this case, Mike is Sally's supervisor and he can never let a document go out without proofreading it in detail first, and in almost every case, there are errors and sloppiness throughout. He has to go through every document with a red pen and make notations in the margins showing Sally where corrections need to be made.

This is frustrating, time-consuming, and not a good use of Mike's time. So the cost of this performance deficiency *can* be expressed in unnecessary labor time, increased cycle time, and lost productivity.

C. Is it worth doing something about?

What do you think? I think yes, since word processing and proofreading are core competencies of Sally's job, not Mike's.

Which brings us to:

E. If you held a gun to her head, could she do what you want her to do?

According to Mike, Sally's accuracy and attention to detail *used* to be fine. It has become progressively worse and worse as time goes on. So, if you held a gun to her head and said, "type the perfect memo!" she should be able to do it. So, the answer is "yes." We know she has the skill because she has done it before. So another way to ask and answer this question is: "Has she ever done it before?" Since the answer is "yes," we now go to:

F. It's a motivation issue.

Obvious. If we know she's able to do it, but she isn't doing it, it isn't a skill issue. It's motivation. For some reason, Sally doesn't see a need to type well any more. What could cause such a change in motivation?

G. Is something else taking priority?

According to Mike, the answer is "no." But it would behoove him to ask Sally as well. Sometimes managers are not aware that something or someone else in the organization may be pulling attention away from their subordinates without their knowledge or awareness or even their permission.

But assuming Mike is right, and the answer is "no," you would then move to an analysis of the consequences of her behavior (Go to "J").

H. Should it be?

If the answer to "G" had been "yes" then you must determine whether the task that is taking priority should or should not be doing so. That's an easy one. You are the manager. If the task that's taking priority shouldn't be, then just set the record straight and get her back on track. You do set the priorities, don't you?

If, however, the task that's taking priority *should* be taking priority over the issue at hand, you must now determine:

I. Is it possible to do both priorities?

Be honest here. It's very tempting, and easy, for managers to say "just do it!" or to make everything a number one priority. That's neither fair nor realistic. If it is not possible for Sally to handle both priorities, then the solution is to find someone else to do one of the tasks, to re-rank the priorities, to find some other way of getting them both done (hire a temp, add to staff, authorize overtime, etc.), or to eliminate one of them altogether.

If the answer is "yes," they can both be done, then we move on to:

J. Are the consequences (+ or –) appropriate?

This is where you get to the heart of the matter. Remember in the preface we said that good managers know how to manage consequences? Well, sometimes it isn't quite as straightforward as it may appear.

We already know that Sally has the skill. We are still trying to determine why she lacks the motivation. Let's see if we can figure out what possible consequence could be causing Sally's behavior. Let's dig a little deeper.

K. Is the desired performance rewarding?

This is where your analysis can get a little sticky. Don't be hasty in your conclusions here. Actually, the desired performance is not particularly rewarding, aside from the personal satisfaction of a job well done, the fact that it is expected as part of her job, and that it should eventually be reflected in her annual performance review. Not too compelling, huh?

But what is a manager to do? Give Sally a reward every time she types an accurate memo? Let's get real! It's not a special project or something above and beyond her basic job requirements. So, the answer here may be "No"—it may not be particularly rewarding, but is that really the root cause here? Keep digging!

L. Establish appropriate rewards.

For the purposes of this example, we would have moved on to M because we are not going to add rewards for basic job expectations. But, if you determined that the desired performance has no positive outcome for the employee, you would try to determine how to build incentives into the equation.

Be careful here, because, as in this example, you do not want to fall into the trap of having to reward core competencies every time an employee does what she is getting paid for in the first place. This section is really more relevant to rewarding those behaviors that may go beyond the basics, or that require additional skills or sacrifice on the part of the employee.

But also remember that this is where you can really get creative. Just stay away from relying too heavily on your compensation system for solutions. It could be something as simple as a pat on the back or public recognition. Make the reward correlate to the behavior. The bigger the behavior, the better the reward.

Now, for this example, let's move on to "M."

M. Is the undesired performance punishing?

So far, no! But Mike is surely ready to find a way to make it so! In other words, when Sally gives Mike a report or project that is sloppy and full of errors, does he beat her mercilessly? Does he cause her great pain? Of course not, but he could do something to make the consequences of her performance start to matter. Here is where the revelation occurs.

Mike decided that it was time to counsel Sally about this issue and to determine why she lacks the motivation to do accurate word processing, particularly since he knows she is capable of doing it. When he asks her why her typing has become so sloppy, her response is, "Well, Mike. No matter what I type, you always change something or make corrections on the draft copy anyway, so why should I waste time concerning myself with producing final quality work when you are going to change it or fix it anyway?"

Think about this. Although there were no immediate rewards for accurate word processing, and no punishment for sloppy word processing, in effect Sally *was* being rewarded for sloppy work. Hmm! She was delegating the task of proofreading and editing upward to her boss, and he fell right into the trap and did it. That's her reward! She got the boss to do her proofreading! Voilá!

So, let's go to:

N. Establish appropriate punishments.

What can Mike do to correct the consequences of Sally's behavior? There are several options, actually. And this is where your discretion and creativity as a manager must come in. The bottom line is that he can no longer continue to "reward" Sally by doing her proofreading and editing for her. And if her sloppiness continues, there should be some form of negative consequence, such as a written warning in her file, a critical incident report to affect her next merit increase, some privilege or perk revoked, etc.

O. Performance expectation counseling required.

Mike must make it clear to Sally that she is paid to do proofreading and editing, and that it is not appropriate nor a good use of his time for him to be doing it for her. He must make it clear that it is his prerogative to change a report or memo after the fact, if he feels it necessary to do so. That does not mean that he is responsible for her quality.

Again, this is where a manager's discretion must be used. Perhaps you give her a verbal warning first—a reality check—and reinforce your faith in her and give her an opportunity to avoid "punishment" first. But make it clear that there will be negative consequences if she does not heed the warning.

In the real world, and once a manager is more adept at the process of managing consequences, this discussion could have and should have taken place during the discussion in "M" when Mike found out what was going on during his diagnostic discussion with Sally. But there is nothing wrong with thinking it through first. Life as a manager is not always "flow-chartable," so understand that one can and should learn how to build the necessary flexibility into the process of analysis, diagnosis, and intervention.

V. Performance improvement?

This one is pretty obvious, but the key point is to follow up and follow through. That which is observed, measured, and rewarded gets done! If Mike drops the ball and does not keep Sally's feet to the fire, or conversely does not recognize her improvement, everything up to now becomes moot. What a waste of time and effort!

If improvement occurs, this is where you can and should come up with an *appropriate* reward. The key word here is "appropriate." Given the nature of this performance discrepancy, a verbal "atta-boy" or "atta-girl" may be sufficient. Or, if you did issue a written warning, you may offer to remove it from her record and give her a clean slate after a sustained period of performance improvement.

If improvement is lacking, you may go back to the drawing board (flowchart) and attempt another approach. But ultimately you have given her the opportunity to perform, she has the ability, and you eventually have no alternative but to remove her from this assignment. Reassignment or termination is warranted.

Just a footnote: As a manager, you should approach performance management with the goal of improving performance and saving an employee, not as a way to "get your ducks in a row" for termination. Many times, managers just want to "build a case" against an employee so he can be terminated and the manager can be protected from potential liability.

Following this flowchart will protect you from unnecessary intervention (remember the lunch hour case?), from making bad decisions (or no decisions), and from illegitimate terminations. But the ultimate goal should be to do what is right, by the employee and by the organization. That is true performance management.

What if it's a skill issue?

The Sally scenario was clearly not a skill issue. She had typed accurately before. But let's look at one that takes a different path through the flowchart. Back to "A."

A. What's the problem?

Customers have complained about their interactions with Mike. They claim he is brash, impatient with their problems or questions, and generally not very "service-oriented" or friendly.

B. What's the cost/benefit?

Since the complaints are coming from more than one customer, it seems apparent that it is not just a personality conflict, or an isolated incident, or due to a particularly difficult customer. The issue has become generalized around Mike and it could easily cost the company customers and goodwill.

C. Is it worth doing something about?

Obviously.

E. If you held a gun to his head, could he do what you want him to do?

The record shows that Mike has been counseled about this before, and he has failed to change or improve in this area. You thought he had the ability to handle a customer service position because he had worked for a competitor in the same type of job before coming to your company. But just because someone had the title, does not mean he has the skills. Maybe that's why he isn't there any longer!

Unfortunately, the counseling either fell on deaf ears, or he just doesn't know what to do differently. Either way, it does not appear to be a motivation issue because he already knows that he is on notice, which leads us to believe there must be some other obstacle preventing him from improving the quality of his customer interactions.

P. It's a skill issue.

Obviously. That's the only choice left.

Q. Can you make it easier to do?

Well, we can't just ask our customers to change their reaction to Mike, and we can't remove the customer interaction from Mike's job, since that *is* his job, so it doesn't appear that simplifying the task is an option.

R. Can he be trained?

Perhaps. But first we must determine if he has already received such training, and if so, why it didn't work. Was it done too long ago? Was it even the right type of training? Was the learning not transferred into improved on-the-job performance? If not, why not?

As you can see, there are more boxes we could have put into the flowchart at this point, but these questions must come from you, and should be obvious in determining if training is a solution. Let's assume for purposes of this example that training is not the solution because he has already been through extensive customer service, communication, and problem-solving training. It was the same training that his peers had received, and they are performing just fine.

> *Training has its limitations. You can't teach a pig to sing. You can't teach a rock to swim.*

S. Can he be transferred?

If the job cannot be made easier to accommodate Mike's deficiencies, and training does not seem to "stick," then there may be no other option but to find another position for Mike. If this is possible, then do it. If not, then:

T. Are you willing/able to buy time?

In other words, can you afford to keep him where he is until something else opens up, or until he just miraculously improves on his own?

That's a decision only you can make. My opinion on this one is that you cannot afford to continue to alienate your customer base to save one employee, particularly since he has already been given sufficient time, tools, and opportunity to succeed.

U. Termination necessary

You have given him every opportunity to succeed; the job requires certain core competencies; he does not have them, nor can he seem to acquire them. In this case, you are in a perfectly justifiable, defensible position to terminate Mike's employment. There is a motto in modern organizational behavior: "You don't terminate people; you terminate behaviors." Sorry, Mike!

Q.R.S.T.

Assuming you did decide that you could either simplify the position requirements (Q), send him to training (R), transfer him (S), or buy time (T), you must still follow up for performance improvement (V) to determine if the problem has been solved, or if you have exhausted all remedies to no avail, thus requiring termination.

Conclusion

All roads eventually lead to performance improvement (V), transfer (S), or termination (U). That may sound rather cold or calloused but it is that simple. How you get to V, S, or U is what matters. Hopefully this map will help you and your employees stay on the road to success in the most fair, equitable, and business-driven manner.

Organizational Change Map

Similar to the Behavioral Change Map, this tool also helps you identify, prioritize, and focus on those things that deserve to be changed and that you have the power to change, and then directs you to the most appropriate avenue for that change. The difference here, however, is that we are addressing organizational change instead of personal behavioral change (Figure 4.2).

As you will also discover, there is a link between this map and the Behavioral Change Map in the event the change requires influencing

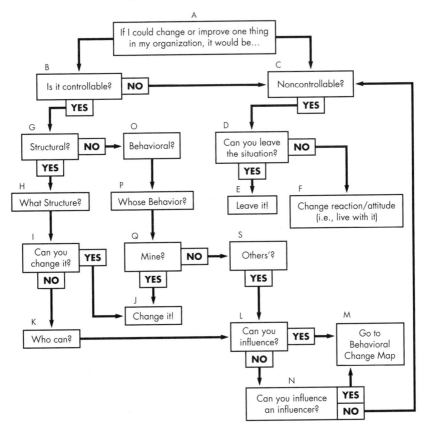

FIGURE 4.2 Organizational Change Map.

another's behavior. In some cases, organizational change is dependent upon individual behavioral change.

The key to any significant organizational change is to be both patient and impatient at the same time.

Additionally, any successful organizational change requires a combination of patience and impatience: patience to maintain stick-to-itiveness and impatience to maintain motivation. It won't usually happen overnight, and it won't happen at all if there is no lasting motivation to make it happen. Knowing that, let's walk through the flowchart.

A. If I could change or improve one thing in my organization, it would be....

This is called The Magic Wand technique. If you could wave a magic wand over your organization and change just one thing, what would it be? The reason you are asked to change only one thing is to force you to prioritize. Similar to the cost-benefit analysis step in the Behavioral Change Map, we must learn to focus our efforts on the most productive and worthy areas.

Although this map can be used for virtually any type of organizational change, the Magic Wand technique is an easy way to identify the most critical issues to attack first.

B. Is it controllable?

Think of this section of the map as an organizational Serenity Prayer. The Serenity Prayer says, "God grant me the serenity to accept the things I cannot change, the courage to change the things I can, and the wisdom to know the difference." If the thing you want to change is controllable, proceed to Box G to further clarify the issue.

However, if it is not controllable, move to Box C.

C. Noncontrollable?

If you answered yes, you only have two options.

D. Can you leave the situation?

In other words, if the situation is one that cannot be changed, one option is to remove yourself from it altogether. For example, let's say you would like to change the geographic location of your employer. Since your employer is not going to pack up and move the company for you, one option is for you to leave the company and find work in a different location if that is so important to you, which is Box E.

E. Leave it!

If the situation is so intolerable, and it cannot be changed, then this option suggests that you divorce yourself from it. Leave! If you decide that is not an option for some reason (maybe there is no work in your field in the location you prefer), then you move to Box F.

F. Change your reaction/attitude—i.e., live with it!

You can't change it! You can't leave it! You can only learn to live with it. It really is that simple. Like it or not, these are your only options, so you have to choose whether to be miserable or to adapt. How you do that is another whole book, but you can choose your attitude. You do have control over that, and it can be changed. So in reality, change is still possible here!

G. Is it structural?

Assuming you said "yes" to the question "Is it controllable?" (B), you must now go to G and determine the type of issue you are addressing. If you say "Yes" to G, "Is it structural?" then define the structure (H). If you say "No" to G, then go to O, which automatically means that it is behavioral. It has to be one or the other.

H. What structure?

For example, is it the organizational structure, reporting relationships, compensation plan, or some other policy, procedure, or non-human entity? Once you identify the specific structure that is the culprit, you must then identify who, if anyone, can change it.

I. Can you change it?

Pretty straightforward here. If you say "Yes" and have the authority and the ability to change it, and it is as important as you claim it is (i.e., it qualified for The Magic Wand treatment), then go to J and *change it!* If you answer "No" and you cannot change it yourself, then proceed to K.

J. Change it!

Rejoice! You've solved the problem! Now go back to the beginning (A) and identify another one! If you answered "No" to Box I "Can You Change It?" go to:

K. Who can?

If you cannot change it, and you stated in B that it is controllable (i.e., that it can be changed), then determine who has the authority or ability to change it, if not you.

L. Can you influence?

Let's say there is a policy or procedure that is driving you nuts or costing your department excessive time or resources, and you do not have purview over it. Does your boss? Does some other department have jurisdiction, like the Legal Department or Human Resources? Ultimately there has to be someone, or some department, that can change anything structural.

Once you determine the focus of influence, ask yourself if there is a way you can sway them to see the merit in changing or eliminating it. Can you do a cost-benefit analysis? Can you administer an attitude survey? Can you conduct a focus group? Then, can you meet with the person of influence and influence him or her? If the answer is "Yes" go to M. If the answer is "No" go to N.

M. Go to Behavioral Change Map

This is where the Behavioral Change Map links to the Organizational Change Map because you are now dealing with individual human behavior in order to change an organizational structure. There are numerous ways to influence those over whom you have no direct control or authority, as mentioned in L above.

Look at the consequences of their behavior, the skill, the motivation, etc. just like we did in the Behavioral Change Map. Assign an organizational cost to not changing it. When all else fails, a little bribery or blackmail is still a viable option! (Just kidding... kinda... depends on how you define bribery and blackmail.) In other words, what's in it for them?

N. Can you influence an influencer?

Assuming again that you were correct in answering "Yes" to B, "Is It Controllable?," then someone has to be able to change it. If you have no influence over the person who is directly responsible for changing it, then is there someone else who does have the ability to influence them whom *you* can influence? Some people call this networking. Some call it politics. Some call it three degrees of separation. Whatever you call it, it is a matter of working your way to the source of the solution, whether directly or indirectly.

If you answer "yes" to N, then you go back to M again, the Behavioral Change Map, and start working the system with this person.

If you answer "no" to N, i.e., you have no influence over anyone who could even indirectly impact the change, then you goofed up or were in denial way back in B, and it really isn't controllable after all! Which takes you back to C, in which you either leave the situation (E) or get over it (F). Sorry! Sometimes reality really stinks!

O. Is it behavioral?

If you said "No" to G, "Is It Structural?" then it has to be behavioral. In other words, if the thing you want to change is not a process, procedure, policy, etc., then it must be a person. If so, go to P.

P. Whose behavior?

Is it your behavior or someone else's? If it is yours, go to J and change it! That was easy! I'm just not sure why you had to wade through this whole map to come to that conclusion!

If it is someone else's behavior, go to S.

S. Others'?

If the issue needing to be changed is behavioral, and it isn't your behavior that is the problem, then it has to be someone else's, so the only possible answer to S is "Yes," which brings you back to L, "Can You Influence?" and so on. You just can't escape this flowchart without some sort of solution, resolution, or conclusion.

Conclusion

There is no escaping reality in this change map. You can't lie and you can't get out of this without finding the truth of the issue, and sometimes it may be you or one of your own structures that is the culprit. Regardless of whether you like the outcome

> *To survive, you must adapt. To succeed, you must initiate!*

or not, it brings focus and resolution to any organizational change issue. When all is said and done, go back to the Serenity Prayer!

AIM to Be Weird

(A Personal Strategy for Integrating Your Abilities, Interests and Markets)

What is one of the first questions someone asks you when you meet for the first time? "What do you do?" And in our society, that translates into "Where do you work?" or "What is your occupation?" If you really want to mess with someone who asks you that question, tell them that you fish, or that you play tennis, or something else that is totally nonoccupational, and I guarantee they will get a strange look on their face, and not know how to proceed with the conversation. Since we seem to be defined by what we do, maybe we should be called human doings instead of human beings.

It took me many years and many mistakes to finally tap my natural weirdness. Fortunately, in my earlier career, I was trained to do outplacement counseling, both large-scale, and one on one. In the process of learning the ropes, and after working with thousands of displaced souls, I came to the realization that there were consistent, recurrent reasons for so many people being so lost in the world of work.

I also saw many of them become highly successful in completely different fields than those from which they were terminated because this was the first time in their lives that someone was asking them the tough questions about their career decisions and qualifications that they should have been asking themselves many years earlier. I saw a truck driver become a stock broker, an engineer become a tour bus operator, and many other wild occupational conversions. Thus, I created this model.

The principal behind this model, commonly known as a Venn Diagram (the intersection of concentric circles), is to guide, develop, and expand one's career choices based upon three critical elements. Those elements are: *A*bilities, *I*nterests, and *M*arkets—thus the acronym *AIM*. Without all three, you will experience something short of a calling or a passion that pays.

Granted, one can get fulfillment without getting paid, but the assumption in this model is that you must work for a living and are looking to maximize both your job satisfaction and your earning potential within a chosen field. Money is not enough of a motivator to make anyone excel at anything over the long haul. Professional sports has proven that! But if you have great Abilities and great Interest in a chosen field, success and its rewards will follow more easily.

If you combine the ultimate need for self-actualization (ref: the highest need based upon Abraham Maslow's Hierarchy of Needs[1])

---

1. Abraham Maslow was a psychologist who proposed a theory of human motivation for understanding behavior based primarily upon a hierarchy of five need categories progressing from basic physiological needs like food and water, to safety and security needs like protection, to love, or social needs, to esteem needs, and ultimately to self-actualization. As a lower need is met, a person progresses to the next higher level of need as a source of motivation, the highest one being self-actualization.

with good old capitalism, it stands to reason that most of us must attempt to satisfy the need for fulfillment in our work. And when we don't, a multitude of negative behavioral outcomes can result.

At one extreme, people can actually die. A number of years ago, Blue Cross/Blue Shield studied death records of people who died while at work. The finding, which has been repeatedly substantiated by subsequent reports, found that the overwhelming majority of people who die on the job die on a Monday. They called this the "Monday Morning Blues." Now that's blue!

Please note that the message here is not that work kills, nor is the message to avoid work altogether. That's called retirement, and it kills too! It is to avoid work that you hate. The reason so many people keel over on Monday is that with all the other pressures of everyday life (financial, marital, physiological, etc.), if you add the stress of dreading the way you spend most of your waking hours— at work—it is on Monday morning that "reality" hits you again and again, particularly if you have to escape it on the weekend.

The resultant recommendation from this research study was that because so many people have to make such a dramatic psychological adjustment on Monday morning from leisure and fun to work, they should try to spread their relaxation and exercise over the entire week, so that Monday is not such an abrupt adjustment. Sounds good, but do these researchers have any ideas on how to do that? Try telling your boss that you need more fun and relaxation time on the job. Work is work, and fun is fun and never the twain shall meet. Or shall they?

Short of death, some seek to find escapes in the form of off-the-job diversions, perversions, drugs, alcohol, or any of a host of other risky or edgy endeavors, as we saw in some of the cases. Others look for their fulfillment "fix" in the form of avocations, hobbies, thrill-seeking activities, volunteering, etc. And we've already talked about the new virtues of "moonlighting," which can also fill that void.

I know an IRS employee who tends bar on weekends, a financial advisor who performs in the theater, a caterer who plays in a rock band, and a CEO who is a moto-cross dirt biker. It's not that these are always attempts to find fulfillment in lieu of their "real jobs," but this trend is becoming more prevalent and more acceptable than ever before.

But the ultimate escape from death by work is to love your work. Few people die as a result of doing what they love, by pursuing their passion, from fulfilling their purpose. So, how can we combine Maslow's self-actualization with capitalism and tap our natural weirdness occupationally?

Let's go through each sector of the Venn diagram piece by piece.

Abilities + Interests = Avocation

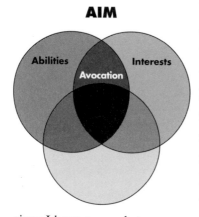

AIM

You can love to do something (Interests), and even be great at it (Abilities), but it's possible that no one is willing to pay you for it (Market). For example, I love to eat, and I am really good at it. But I have yet to find someone to pay me for it. Or, if no one bought this book, even if I love to write, and am good at it, my writing would only be an avocation, since I have no market.

On a more serious note, many people default to this sector of the diagram (pursue an avocation) as an escape from their real "work." In other words, you may not love your job, but you love the theater. You may act in local plays, but it is not a career for you. It is an intrinsically rewarding escape (Avocation) where you are able to use both your interests and your abilities.

There is nothing wrong with that. But wouldn't it be wonderful to be able to escape into your work? Wouldn't it be wonderful to get paid for what you love and can do well? After all, work is where most of us spend most of our waking hours!

Interests + Market = Dream

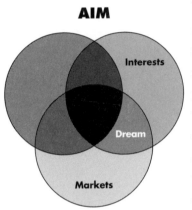

AIM

Who hasn't dreamed of being a movie star, a professional athlete, a concert musician, a racecar driver? There are markets for these talents. But you probably *ain't no good* at these things! Sorry to be so blunt, but someone had to tell you! OK, maybe you aren't of the caliber to be able to do them for a living. In any event, it's a dream. Time to wake up!

Sadly, there actually are people who attempt to work in careers in which their talents aren't suited. That's painful ... for everyone. They may even get by for a while, but it certainly isn't rewarding for them or their employer, and eventually something or someone has to give. Whether it's a stress-related ailment, career outplacement, or unhealthy escapes, nothing really good can come out of it in the long run.

There are numerous reasons why people go into jobs that don't suit their abilities. From idealism to parental pressure to misguided career counseling to over-emphasis on pay scales, the bottom line is that this is not an ideal place to be, and it will catch up to them. And the sooner the better, so they will still have time to take AIM.

Abilities + Markets = Job

So, what's wrong with that? You're good at something, and they pay you for it! Without the Interest, motivation and satisfaction will always be lacking. It's just a job. A hard job! Ultimately, if you are not fired with enthusiasm, you will probably be fired, with enthusiasm.

AIM

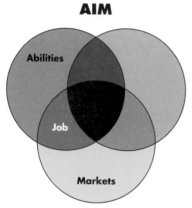

Again, paychecks don't drive you out of bed in the morning. Paychecks don't make you want to excel every day. Paychecks don't make you feel centered in life. Just as in the Dream mode (Interests + Market), this will also eventually catch up to you, and in the exact same way in the forms of stress, job loss, addictions, bitterness, mediocrity, and other negative outcomes.

Abilities + Interests + Market = Target for Success

AIM

You're good at something, you love it, and they pay you for it! It doesn't get any better than this! These are the people that every employer wants to hire and are sometimes the weirdos in the workplace that this book cherishes—the ones rooted in genius and high performance.

They have tapped their natural weirdness to the max, and life is good. They jump out of bed in the morning, or maybe even in the middle of the night, anxious to take on another day. Most of this book was written at 3:00 in the morning. Not just because I had a passion, but I had a job to do too!

In the context of this book, at its extreme, these are the people referred to as "high-performance weirdos" and for whom the section entitled "What's IN With High-Performers?" is intended. The more people find their niche in the world of work, the more they require and even demand these five needs be met.

There are plenty of historic and modern day examples of people from all walks of life, past and present, who have reached their pinnacle, or self-actualization: Notable figures already mentioned like Albert Einstein and Thomas Edison, and others like Bill Gates, Tiger Woods, Walt Disney, Robin Williams, Michael Jordan, and many more that you can probably think of. They have gone beyond self-esteem. Attaining self-actualization means that you have actually found your purpose in life, your reason for being. You are fulfilling it and it is fulfilling you. And it can get weird.

Sound too idealistic? Maybe. But why not at least be AIMing for it? At least you would be heading in the right direction! How do you do that? Well, you have to know yourself. Sounds simple, but it isn't. Here are some examples and exercises to get you AIMed on the road to natural weirdness and success.

Abilities

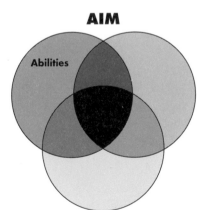

AIM

Abilities

What are your skills? Seems like a simple question, but it is amazing how few people can really answer that question honestly or accurately for themselves. Here's the first question you must ask yourself to get started identifying your abilities: "What have I accomplished thus far in my life?"

This is not some rhetorical or mystical question. Think about all of your past jobs, volunteer assignments, hobbies, and personal endeavors, and think about what you are the most proud of having accomplished. It doesn't have to be occupational. You didn't even have to get paid for it. You may have led the most successful fund-raiser for the church. You may have mentored a child at risk. You may have just re-organized the office closet. It doesn't matter how grandiose it is; it's something you did well!

This is not an easy assignment. In fact, in my counseling days, this was the most difficult part of the process for most people, because they were too humble, underestimated themselves, took their accomplishments for granted, or assumed that since they did not have a big fancy job title, that they were not in a position to accomplish anything. Bull-oney!

One technique for writing your accomplishment statements is to think of the acronym STAR again. Only this time, you are to identify a **S**ituation or **T**ask with which you were confronted. Write it down! Then write down the **A**ction(s) you took, followed by the **R**esult(s). Putting your accomplishments into this context can help you see the cause and effect relationships of any challenges with which you succeeded and the skills it required to do so. Do not stop this process until you have documented at least ten accomplishments, no matter how mundane they may seem to you. If you need something to jog your brain, turn to the List of Action Verbs on pages 169–170.

Next, take another piece of paper and, one by one, look at each accomplishment and ask yourself, "What skill/ability did I need to do this?" (For help here, see the Transferable Skills List on page 170–171.) If you mentored a child, you had to have strong listening, empathy, and interpersonal skills. If you raised funds for the church, you had to have strong sales, persuasion, and influence skills. If you organized a storage closet, you had to have strong initiative, organizational, and prioritizing skills. It doesn't matter what the task, it takes some sort of skill to do it.

As you go through each accomplishment, you will begin to see similar skills popping up over and over. That's the whole point. Don't gloss over this. *Look for repeats.* Either write the skill a second and third and fourth time, or put hash marks beside the skill every time it appears, but the point is to start finding your skill clusters. Then rank them.

When you are done with this, you will *absolutely* know your Abilities. Then, when someone asks the question, "What are your strengths?" you now have an answer that is rooted in the truth with real-life examples and accomplishments to back it up. Could come in handy in a job interview, huh?

Interests

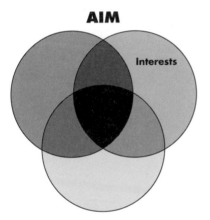

AIM

Interests

What do you like? Another simple-sounding question. Can you answer it? Can you answer it accurately and honestly? Well, let's make sure you can.

Go back to your list of former employers and other experiences from the prior exercise. Now draw a line down the center of a blank piece of paper and a line across the top like a T-chart or balance sheet. On the top left header, write the word "Liked" and on the top right header, write the word "Disliked."

Now go back in your mind and recall what you really liked and disliked about as many former jobs or volunteer experiences as you can. Again, do not avoid repeating yourself. That's the whole point again! Repetition is revelation.

If you find that "poor communication" was a dislike in several former jobs, then keep writing it down or making hash marks beside it, and when you're done you'll know that this is very important to you. You are interested in working in an environment in which they practice open book management, or in which they share the bigger picture with people, etc. If you find that you enjoyed customer interaction and solving problems, then you know that it's important that you have interaction and challenge.

When you are done with this exercise, you will be able to define the ideal work environment for you, in terms of the nature of the work and the culture of the organization. Now when you are asked to describe the ideal job, you can answer with pizzazz and preciseness. Again, could come in handy in a job interview!

Markets

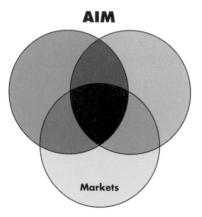

AIM

Markets

Unfortunately, this one is completely up to you. It is not possible within the context of this book to identify every market opportunity, nor to list every resource. There are lots of other good books out there on this topic. But if you have a complete handle on your Abilities and your Interests, the Markets should be relatively easy to identify. In fact, they should just pop out at you.

The key point here is to think of yourself *not* as a job title or even in terms of a particular occupation. In other words, you are not just an accountant. You may be an accountant with strong sales and influence skills. You are not just an engineer. You may be an engineer with a flair for the creative and innovative. Once you have identified your abilities and interests, you can merge them into a powerful, and real, personal statement.

Abilities and interests are transferable across a multitude of occupations and industries. Accountants can go into sales. They can sell accounting software, financial services, or even themselves as independent consultants. Engineers can go into creative fields like graphic design or visual arts. For examples of transferable skills, go to the Transferable Skills list on page 170–171.

Last and certainly not least, if you look at the Venn diagram, you will realize that the larger any one or more of the circles is, the larger your target of opportunity becomes. For instance, as you acquire or identify new abilities, that circle gets larger and therefore the overlap gets larger. As your interests broaden, that circle gets larger and the overlap gets larger. You may not be able to control the market, but you can take a larger bite out of it.

Those who are multitalented with diverse interests have more options. The larger the target, the greater your potential for hitting it. And once you find the intersection of your abilities, your interests, and the market, you will be on the road to tapping your natural weirdness. You will be a weirdo to be loved and richly rewarded!

Action Verbs for Accomplishments

Accelerated	Converted	Facilitated
Accomplished	Coordinated	Forecasted
Achieved	Created	Formulated
Administered	Cut	Headed
Analyzed	Delegated	Generated
Approved	Delivered	Identified
Audited	Demonstrated	Implemented
Authored	Designed	Improved
Budgeted	Developed	Improvised
Built	Devised	Initiated
Completed	Directed	Increased
Conceived	Eliminated	Innovated
Conducted	Established	Installed
Consolidated	Evaluated	Instituted
Controlled	Expanded	Introduced

Invented	Purchased	Structured
Investigated	Recommended	Summarized
Launched	Recruited	Supervised
Lead	Redesigned	Systematized
Maintained	Reduced	Taught
Managed	Reorganized	Terminated
Mediated	Researched	Traced
Mentored	Resolved	Tracked
Motivated	Revised	Trained
Negotiated	Scheduled	Transferred
Operated	Serviced	Transformed
Organized	Settled	Translated
Performed	Set up	Trimmed
Planned	Simplified	Tracked
Presented	Sold	Uncovered
Processed	Solved	Utilized
Produced	Staffed	Verified
Proposed	Started	Worked
Programmed	Streamlined	Wrote
Promoted	Strengthened	
Provided	Stretched	

Transferable Skills

Administrative	Conceptual	Decision-Making
Analytical	Conflict-Resolution	Delegation
Budgeting	Coordination	Design
Coaching	Counseling	Developmental
Communication	Creative Thinking	Diplomacy

Evaluating	Mediating	Scheduling
Facilitative	Mentoring	Staffing
Forecasting	Motivational	Social
Fund-Raising	Negotiating	Streamlining
Goal-Setting	Organizational	Supervisory
Initiative	Performance Management	Teaching
Interpersonal	Persuasion	Team Building
Intuition	Planning	Team Leading
Investigative	Political	Technical
Leadership	Problem-Solving	Troubleshooting
Liaison	Recruiting	Understanding
Listening	Revising	Valuing
Management	Selling	Vision

Conclusions
and
Universal Truths

Chapter 5 ———

CONCLUSIONS AND
UNIVERSAL TRUTHS

Conclusions

OK, so what have we learned? Hopefully, quite a few things, but if we summed it all up, the first requirement to thriving in the Age of the Individual is to understand that it demands a multi-faceted approach: changing others, changing organizations, and changing yourself, where warranted.

The cases and analyses represented a full spectrum of real-life examples of workplace behaviors demonstrating everything from nuisance to brilliance, and were an instructional set-up for learning when and how it may be appropriate to intervene. The tool to guide you through this process is the Behavioral Change Map, to determine 1) if the behavior is really a problem worth solving, 2) if it is rooted in a skill deficiency or a lack of motivation, and 3) what intervention alternative will be most effective.

"What's IN With High-Performers" defines the perfect organizational environment needed to target and capitalize on the free agent, rare-talent sector, and how to tailor your culture to those weirdos who bring the most value to the workplace—a key success factor of the Age of the Individual. And the tool for getting there is the Organizational Change Map, to determine 1) what really needs changing, 2) whether it can be changed, and 3) if it is structural or behavioral in cause.

Finally, you can attempt to change others and you can attempt to change organizations, but ultimately, the only thing over which you have direct, immediate, and total control is yourself, and that is where AIM comes in. In fact, regardless of your success at changing others or your organization, you will be assured a greater degree of success and fulfillment in any environment if you are performing at the intersection of your abilities, your interests and the market.

Universal Truths

Universal Truth #1: "As Goes the World, So Goes the Workplace!"

Coming full circle, we covered this universal truth in detail in Chapter 1. But it is *the* underlying principal behind understanding where we've been, how we got where we are, and where we are going as a society and therefore in the workplace. It is a never-ending process, so keep your eye on the ball. It doesn't stop. To paraphrase former hockey star and scoring genius Wayne Gretzky, "The key to success is not skating to where the puck is, but to where it is going to be."

It's actually quite fascinating to watch how accurate this universal truth is, once you start making the translations on your own. If you don't already, start keeping abreast of societal, economic, religious, political, global and other trends (not fads), and you will literally be able to predict and anticipate what you can expect to see as future workplace evolutions occur, and to get ahead of the curve both professionally and personally.

Watch the news. The real news. Read the journals, keep your hand on the pulse of society, and many of the changes and challenges with which you will be faced will come as no surprise. Eventually you will no longer have to react, but can start predicting and pro-acting, which not only gives you more control, but less stress, and will make you more valuable to any organization.

Universal Truth #2: "The More You're Worth, the More You Can Be Weird!"

The more valuable an individual is to society, to an organization, or even to a partner, the more willingness there is to accommodate or even ignore his or her weirdness. Remember the examples of professional athletes, actors, musicians, and artists who are known to be eccentric, demanding, and almost intolerable at times?

Some people can get away with murder, literally, because society has decided that they have earned that level of forgiveness or amnesty. Right or wrong, our society places very disparate formulas to individuals' behaviors in assessing penalties for indiscretions, faulty moral or ethical compasses, conflicts of interest, deviant behavior, and the like, based upon the perceived value of the individual.

Philosophically and historically, varying degrees of punishment and forgiveness are supposed to be proportionate to the nature and severity of the crime and one's past record, but in the Age of the Individual, they are now also dependent upon the offender's relative status in his or her organization or in society at large.

The converse is also true. Once the negative impact of an individual's weirdness on others exceeds his or her perceived value or performance, the net gain is zero or negative, resulting in the weirdo being less worthy of continued tolerance or accommodation. Again, it boils down to a pure cost-benefit proposition. When more is lost by the collective impact or distraction on others than the weirdo's value can off-set, the game changes. Essentially, tolerance of weirdness becomes a function of gain versus pain. *That's the Weird/Worth Ratio!*

Can you think of "has been" actors who have to take bit parts or appear as paid endorsers on infomercials just to pay the bills and/or to maintain any sort of public persona? Or politicians who have lost their power base who can no longer command an audience with influential higher ups or negotiate big deals? Or formerly high-powered execu-tives, whose behaviors have subjected their organizations to the scru-tiny of the media and legal microscopes, who used to be able to command jets to their personal resorts for extravagances beyond the pale of "normal" people, but now can't even get a return phone call?

Individual value, perceived or real, can offset a certain degree of weirdness if there is a net gain to those who must tolerate it or on whom the weirdo is dependent. And again, this concept is not just rele-vant to organizations. That is what makes it a *universal* truth. We apply it to husbands, wives, partners, children, friends, and anyone else with whom we must associate and negotiate every day. It may be painful to admit, but it is the truth.

As you saw in the analyses of the cases, those who brought a lot to the game deserved a little more consideration and accommodation than those who were just an annoyance or offensive. This is not only legal, but it is essential. To repeat the mantra one more time, "Discrimination is good, it is right, and it is necessary ... based on performance and value."

That's why the AIM concept is so important if you want to increase your market value as an individual. To be a weirdo of worth and to capitalize on it, you must identify and maximize it. If you think like a free agent, then you must act like one, which means that you are only worth as much as you bring to the game.

And once we have maximized the ability and the value of the indi-vidual, and everyone is in the right place doing the right thing, for them, the perception of weirdos in the workplace will evolve to the point where…

Universal Truth #3: "The More Weirdos There Are, the Fewer There Are!"

This is where the STAR progression comes in. As we now know, every organization and every individual falls somewhere in this sequence as it relates to the Age of the Individual. Do you **St**ifle, **T**olerate, **A**ccept, or **Re**joice in weirdos in the workplace? Where does your organization fall in this progression?

To review, traditional organizations tried to Stifle individuals from exerting their individuality, motivated by a need for command and control. Sameness, loyalty, and harmony ruled the day. Then we were forced to accommodate formerly excluded groups of people under the umbrella of diversity (race, sex, etc.), requiring a new Tolerance. But as our economy shifted to one requiring more creativity and innovation, and demand for talent exceeded supply, we had no choice but to learn to start Accepting what goes along with hiring oddballs.

> *The only "normal" people are the ones you just don't know yet.*

And we even learned to live with them, particularly since they started to prove valuable.

But the only way to attain a true and lasting culture of high performance weirdness is to **R**ecognize, **R**eward, and **R**ejoice in the value of weirdos in the workplace. In the Age of the Individual, everyone is a weirdo and no one is a weirdo. The ultimate and perhaps almost utopian goal for an organization, and for society, is for everyone to be reaping the rewards of tapping his or her natural weirdness as was detailed in Chapter 4 (AIM to Be Weird), in which case the concept of "weird" becomes the "norm." In other words, "the more weirdos there are, the fewer there are!"

Coming full circle, diversity is individuality. Weirdness is a perception. Value is relative. Understanding of self and others are the elixir for living peacefully and successfully with Weirdos in the Workplace, and Thriving in the Age of the Individual.

Now go Get Weird!

ABOUT THE AUTHOR

John Putzier, M.S., SPHR, is the best-selling author of *Get Weird! 101 Innovative Ways to Make Your Company a Great Place to Work* which was nominated for Book of the Year by the Society for Human Resource Management, was listed as "New & Noteworthy" by Barnes & Noble, was identified as a "Top Ten Must Read" by online reviewer AchieveMax, and received a consistent 5-star rating on Amazon.com.

He is also President of FirStep, Inc., a performance improvement consultancy based in Prospect, PA, which he founded in 1985. He is also the founder and past President of the National Speakers Association–Pittsburgh and founder and past President of the Society for Human Resource Management High-Tech-Net.

Prior to forming FirStep, Inc., John worked in both the public and private sectors, including a decade with a Fortune 100 corporation, where he served as an Equal Employment Opportunity Officer and Manager of Employment, in a variety of human resources positions.

Subsequently, John was a member of the adjunct faculty of Robert Morris University and Carnegie Mellon University's H. John Heinz III Graduate School of Public Policy and Management, where he taught Organizational Behavior and Theory, and has served on a variety of boards of directors of professional associations.

He has a Bachelor of Science in Industrial Psychology (cum laude) from the University of Akron and graduated first in his class from The American University, Washington, D.C., with a Master of Science in Human Resource Development.

John appears regularly in the media as an expert on current and emerging workplace issues and trends, including CNN, *Time*, *USA Today*, *The Wall Street Journal*, *Business Week*, *The New York Times*, *The Washington Post*, and many other publications, radio, and TV programs.

For more information on John's keynote presentations and other business advisory services, go to *www.getweird.net*; call toll free: 1-866-GET WEIRD! (438-9347) or email john@getweird.net.

WEIRDISMS

"A weirdo is anyone not like you, which is why there are so many of them out there."

"The more weirdos there are, the fewer there are!"

"Success comes from good judgment; good judgment comes from experience; and experience comes from bad judgment."

"The only normal people are the ones you just don't know yet."

"Most jerks at work are not born, they are created."

"Everyone behaves perfectly rationally ... from their point of view."

"Decision-making is easy when you have strong values, good or bad!"

"Training has its limitations.... You can't teach a pig to sing ... you can't teach a rock to swim."

"If you hire misfits and just train them, all you have is a bunch of trained misfits."

"Even a dead body will move in a river that is flowing."

"Even a turkey can fly in a tornado."

"It's better to train people and have them leave, than to not train them and have them stay."

"There is always a talent shortage."

"If smart managers always hire people smarter than themselves, wouldn't that mean that the dumbest people are at the top?"

"A paycheck is like breathing.... You take it for granted until it stops."

"How come no one notices what I do around here until I stop doing it?"

"The ultimate escape from death by work is to love your work."

"If the opposite of pro is con, wouldn't the opposite of progress be Congress?

"Every manager must be a human resource manager."

"If you think you can change people, then you haven't been married."

"Hope without 'how' is just an empty promise."

"If today's workers are so disloyal, why can't you steal them from the competition too?"

"If two people in an organization agree on everything, one of them probably isn't needed."

"On the surface, some people are very deep; but deep down, they are very superficial."

"Discrimination is good; discrimination is right; discrimination is necessary if it is based on performance/value."

"The key to successful change is to be both patient and impatient at the same time."

"Why is the road most traveled so popular?"

"Why is ignorance more contagious than intelligence?"

"If expectations create realities, why can't you fake them?"

"If opposites attract, why do birds of a feather flock together?"

"Which is worse ... ignorance or apathy? I don't know and I don't care."

"I can't stand people who are intolerant."

"If non-conformists only associate with other non-conformists, doesn't that make them conformists?"

"Character is what you do when no one is looking."

"That which is observed, measured, and rewarded gets done."

"There is no 'I' in team, but there ain't no 'we' either."

"You can increase your credibility by admitting your fallibility."

"You can judge a man by the way he treats people who can do nothing for him."

"Stand for something, or you will fall for anything."

"I'd rather die standing, than live on my knees."

"To survive, you must adapt. To succeed, you must initiate!"

"If you're not fired with enthusiasm, you will probably be fired, with enthusiasm."

"People don't care how much you know until they know how much you care."

"You can tame a fanatic, but you can't breathe life into a corpse."

"Individuality minus tolerance equals chaos."

"Judgmentalism minus self reflection equals bigotry."

"Trust is the enemy of bureaucracy."

"One-way communication is telling, but two-way communication is liberating."

"Without a reason, there is no motivation."

"All workers are *not* created equal."

"Don't Act ... Become!"

INDEX

A

Abilities *see* AIM
Action Verbs List, 169–170
  use of, 166
Adaptive progression, *see* STAR
Age of Diversity, 6–8, 179
Age of the Individual, 10–12, 179
  including reasons in new motivational model, 122
  and meritocracy, 123
  requirements for, 175
  and resource deployment issues, 13–14
Age of the New Economy, 8–10, 179
Agnes (freedom *from* religion), 33
AIM (Abilities/Interests/Markets), 19, 107, 159–160, 176
  abilities, 165–167
    use of Action Verbs List, 166

    use of Transferable Skills List, 166
  and Behavioral Change Map, 40n
  case example (**A**bility/**I**nterest), 40
  interests, 167–168
  markets, 168–170, 178
  model (Venn Diagram), 160, 160f
  self-actualization and work, 160–162
  see also Avocation; Dream; Job; Target for success
Al Naturale, 43–46, 53, 90, 110
Alex (suspected drug abuse), 79–84
Annie (pet person), 87–88
Assignment characteristics enhancing self-direction, 116
  autonomy, 117
  feedback, 117
  skill variety, 116
  task identity, 116
  task significance, 116
Avocation, 162–163

187

B

Behavioral Change Map, 139, 140f, 141, 175
  and AIM Diagram, 40n
  and analysis of CEO behavior/ consequences (case example), 37
  and analysis of inappropriate stress-management behavior (case example), 65
  case example, 27f
  cost/benefit analysis, 142
  and counseling/termination decisions, 36, 152
  follow through requirements, 148–149
  intervention decision, 142–143, 144
  links to Organizational Change Map, 157
  motivation vs. skill decision (case examples), 38–40, 39f, 54–56, 55f, 144, 150
    intervening priority query (case examples), 144–145
    managing consequences (case example), 145
    punishment issues, 147–148
    reward issues (case example), 146
  performance expectation counseling, 148
  problem identification (case examples), 141–142, 143, 149
  skills issue investigation (case example), 151
Ben the Baptist, 32–33

BFOQ (bona fide occupational qualification), 51–52
Blue Suit Bob, 26–29, 110
Boy Named Sue, 29–32
Buford (confederate supporter), 91–92

C

Case studies
  abused employee (personal life issues)/problem description, 54
    analysis, 54–58
  approach, 25–26
  body art issues problem description, 48–49
    analysis, 49
  body odor issues problem description, 43–44
    analysis, 44–45
    religious expression dimension, 45–46
  breast milk expression problem description, 58
    analysis, 59
  cliques promoting discrimination in the workplace problem description, 52–53
    analysis, 53–54
  close-to-the-vest problem description, 41
    analysis, 42–43
  difficult customer problem description, 84–85
    analysis, 85–87
  disability claims/system abuse problem description, 71–72
    analysis, 72–73

drug use (suspicion of) problem
   description, 79
   analysis (drug testing
      approach), 80–81
   analysis (job performance
      approach), 81–84
employee favoritism based on
   sexual favors problem
   description, 59–61
   analysis, 61–63
exaggerated fears based on work
   situation problem description, 63
   analysis, 63–64
excessive chatting problem
   description, 46–47
   analysis, 47–48
excessive involvement with pets
   problem description, 87
   analysis, 88
expense account charges problem description, 76–78
   analysis, 78
Feng Shui obsession at work
   problem description, 97–99
   analysis, 99
freedom *from* religion problem
   description, 33
   analysis, 33
gender discrimination problem
   description, 31
   analysis, 31–32
gender-reassignment problem
   description, 29
   analysis, 30–31
hypochondria and health focus
   problem description, 88–89
   analysis, 89
inappropriate stress-management
   techniques problem
   description, 64–65

analysis, 65–66
Internet usage (personal vs. business) problem description,
   73–74
   analysis, 74–76
noncompliance with company
   values problem description, 49–50
   analysis, 51–52
off-duty behavior (moonlighting)
   problem description, 34
   analysis, 34–36, 37
off-duty behavior (moonlighting)
   problem description/CEO
   in involvement, 36
   analysis, 36–37
office romance problem description, 66–67
   analysis, 67–69
public campaigning/"advertising"
   problem description, 89–90
   analysis, 90–91
racist political positions problem
   description, 91
   analysis, 92
same outfits problem description,
   27–28
   analysis, 27–29, 27f
solicitations problem description, 69–70
   analysis, 70–71
system-testing/envelope pushing
   problem description, 92–94
tactlessness issues problem
   description, 37–38
   analysis, 38–40, 39f
time-shifting/creative cycles out
   of sync with work hours
   problem
   description, 99–101
   analysis, 101–102

work refusal on religious grounds
    problem description, 32
  analysis, 32–33
worker/boss friction problem
    description, 96–97
  analysis, 97
Chatty Cathy, 46–48
Christine (Carpal Tunnel), 71–73
Circadian Charlie, 99–102, 110, 115
"Composite career," 109
Conflict, benefits of, 119
Consensual-relationship agreements,
  69
Contingency theory, 20
Corporate Equality Index, 32
"Counseling sandwich approach,"
  86
"Creative dissatisfaction," 95
Creativity
  in Age of the New Economy, 10
  and conflict, 119–120
  source in '50s and '60s, 5
Crime at work, 57

D

"Discretionary Effort," 127
Discrimination, 15, 18–19, 141
  special exceptions *see* BFOQ
    (bona fide occupational
    qualification)
Diversity
  and Age of the Individual, 10
  and body-odor issues case exam-
    ple, 44–46
  vs. individualism, 107
  and laissez-faire management
    style, 15
  and "protected classes," 7

self-inflicted (body art) case
    example, 49
and talent, 9
Dream, 163
Drug testing, 76, 80–81
  negative aspects of, 82–83

E

Edison, Thomas, 16
Einstein, Albert, 16
Electronic Communications Privacy
  Act, 74
Elizabeth ("Betty Boop" moonlight-
  ing), 34–37
Elvis, 16
Employer resources
  Dale Carnegie course, 38
  Employee Assistance Program
    (EAP), 55
  Internet usage policies, 75–76
  Job Accommodation Network
    (U.S. Department of
    Labor), 45
  La Leche League, 59
  Occupational Safety and Health
    Administration (OSHA), 64
  personal performance coach,
    65–66
  restraining orders, 57
  SCORE (Service Corps of
    Retired Executives), 39
  white noise, 47–48

F

Feng Shui Phoebe, 97–99
Free Agent Nation, 9, 12
Freedoms as worker value, 113

G

GLBT (Gay, Lesbian; Bisexual; and Transgender) nondiscrimination policies, 32
Google, hiring practices, 17
"Grapevine" management, 35

H

Helen the hypochondriac, 88–89
High performers, 15
    and low-performers, 126
    needs of, 105–106
    and organizational design, 105, 135–136
    and "self-efficacy," 17–18
    and "self-monitoring" behavior, 16
    see also Incentives; Independence; Individualism; Information; Innovation
Hoof-in-Mouth Hal, 37–40
Human billboards, 89–91
Human Resources, origins of, 7
Human Rights Campaign (HRC), 32

I

Incentives, 122
    celebrations, 128–129
    intolerance of low performance, 126
    intrinsically motivating work, 127–128
    nontraditional, 124–126
    pay for performance, 122–124
    "trophy value," 125
Independence, 113
    freedoms as central value, 113
    and goal orientation, 115
    leadership vs. management, 114–115
    reduce bureaucracy, 114
    self-direction of assignments, 116–117
Individualism, 106
    and high-performers as "weirdos," 106–107
    knowing/using strengths, 107–108
    substance over style, 110–111
    and workplace flexibility, 109
    and workplace personal space, 113
Information, 117
    "open book management philosophy," 117, 119
    and positive conflict, 119–120
    real vs. bureaucratic channels of communication, 119
    two-way communication, 118
    "why" as motivator, 120–122
Innovation, 129
    change initiation, 132–133
    environmental conditions, 133–134
    error tolerance, 131–132
    and new technology, 129–131
    synergy from high-performers' interaction, 134–135
Interests see AIM
Internal attribution see Self-efficacy
Intervention costs, 28

J

Jack (play.com), 73–76
Jackson, Michael, 16

Job, 163–164
Job Accommodation Network (U.S. Department of Labor), 45

K

Kelleher, Herb, 16

L

Lacy (breast feeder), 58–59
Lizzie (unrealistic perception of health risks), 63–64
Loretta and Lou (office affair), 59–63
Loyalty, 5, 8
    to profession, 9
Lucretia (perpetually dissatisfied customer), 84–87

M

Magic Wand Technique *see* Organizational Change Map
"Management" vs. "leadership," 114–115
Markets *see* AIM
Mary (values in opposition to products/clients), 49–52
Maslow, Abraham, 160
Meritocracy, and equality, 123
Monday Morning Blues, 161
Moonlighting, 109
Motivation, "why" (reasons) as motivator, 120–122

N

National Public Radio (NPR), workplace romance example, 68
Networking, 157
"New normal," 21–22

O

Office romances, 67
    case example, 66–67
    company policy examples, 68
Open book management philosophy, 117
Organization Man, 5–6, 179
    Age of, 113
    creativity vs. loyalty/harmony, 5
    and new technology, 131
Organizational Change Map, 153–154, 153f, 176
    analysis of controllability, 154
        behavioral change choice, 158
        choices for unchangeable situations, 155
        structural change choices, 155–157
    links to Behavioral Change Map, 157
    Magic Wand technique, 154
    solution/resolution/conclusion, 158–159
Organizational design features for high-performance, 105, 135–136, 176
    incentives, 122
        celebrations, 128
        intolerance of low-performers, 126
        intrinsically motivating work, 127–128

nontraditional, 124–126

pay for performance, 122–124

independence requirements, 113

goal orientation, 115

leadership vs. management, 114–115

reduce bureaucracy, 114

structure assignments for self-direction, 116–117

value freedoms, 113

individualism requirements, 106

allow individual expression in personal space, 112

focus on substance not style, 110–111

foster individualism, 107

foster tolerance, 108

offer flexibility, 109

information requirements, 117

depersonalized conflict opportunities, 119–120

"open book management" philosophy, 117

real vs. bureaucratic communication, 119

reasons for change/challenge, 120–122

two-way communication, 118

innovation, 129

change initiation opportunities, 132–133

encourage interaction among high-performers, 134–135

environment for, 133–134

error tolerance, 131–132

new technology, 129–131

Otto versus Oblivious, 96–97

P

Performance management

goal of, 149

training limitations, 151

Political correctness, 15, 22

Priscilla (on-job charity solicitations), 69–71

Psychological testing/profiling, appropriateness of (case example), 42

Public Affairs (Hank/Hanna office romance), 67–69

R

Realistic Job Preview (RJP), 51

Recruitment tools

psychological testing/profiling, 42

Realistic Job Preview (RJP), 51

Religious expression and workplace issues, 32–33, 45–46

Richard (expense account abuse), 76–78

Rodney ("close to the vest" mentality), 41–43

S

Scientific Management, 113

Self-actualization, 160–162, 165

Self-efficacy, 11, 17–18

Self-monitoring, 16, 107–108

"Sentinel Effect," 76

Sex discrimination, and gender reassignment, 31–32

Sexual harassment, 50, 59
  "consensual-relationship agree-
    ments," 69
  training/awareness, 30–31
Southwest Airlines, "Love Award,"
  68
STAR (adaptive progression), 4, 179
  accepting *see* Age of the New
    Economy
  rejoicing *see* Age of the Individual
  stifling *see* Organization Man
  tolerating *see* Age of Diversity
STAR (Situation/Task/Action(s)/
  Result), 166
Stern, Howard, 16
Style versus substance, 110–111
Suzy (abused/confused), 54–58
"System slop," 75
System Tester Sam, 92–96, 114,
  120, 133

T

Talent
  and free-agent mentality, 12–13
  see also High performers
Target for success, 164–165
Team building
  in '50s and '60s, 5, 10
  and American character, 11–12
  marginalization of, 10–11
  vs. "nerd camaraderie," 135

Technology, and exodus of Organi-
  zation Man, 8
Termination, 152
Terry (ticks/twitches), 64–66
Transferrable Skills List, 170–171
  use of, 166, 168
Trophy value, 125
Trust, 114, 117, 119, 130
  and policy review (case example),
    143
Turnover, benefits of, 124

W

Walking Art, 48–49, 90
Weirdo, 3, 21, 106
  in after-hours interests of
    employees, 17
  as characteristic of high-perform-
    ers, 106–107
  as norm, 179–180
  and self-efficacy, 17–18
  and self-monitoring behavior, 16
  and synergistic/narcissistic
    boundary, 135–136
  and value, 13, 177–179
Weirdo/Worth ratio, 177–178
Whistleblower laws, 118
Workplace, and personal space, 112
Workplace as social microcosm, 4,
  176–177
  melting pot vs. stir-fry, 14